Henry Alford

How to study the New Testament

The Epistles (First section)

Henry Alford

How to study the New Testament
The Epistles (First section)

ISBN/EAN: 9783337257682

Printed in Europe, USA, Canada, Australia, Japan

Cover: Foto ©Lupo / pixelio.de

More available books at **www.hansebooks.com**

HOW TO STUDY THE
NEW TESTAMENT

HOW TO STUDY THE NEW TESTAMENT

THE EPISTLES (FIRST SECTION)

BY HENRY ALFORD, D.D.
DEAN OF CANTERBURY

STRAHAN AND CO., PUBLISHERS
56, LUDGATE HILL, LONDON
1868

PRINTED BY W. CLOWES AND SONS, STAMFORD STREET
AND CHARING CROSS.

CONTENTS.

THE EPISTLES.

		PAGE
I.	INTRODUCTORY	1
II.	THE FIRST EPISTLE TO THE THESSALONIANS	25
III.	THE SECOND EPISTLE TO THE THESSALONIANS	53
IV.	THE FIRST EPISTLE TO THE CORINTHIANS	77
V.	THE SECOND EPISTLE TO THE CORINTHIANS	109
VI.	THE EPISTLE TO THE GALATIANS	134
VII.	THE EPISTLE TO THE ROMANS *(First Part.)*	157
VIII.	THE EPISTLE TO THE ROMANS *(Second Part.)*	179
IX.	THE EPISTLE TO THE COLOSSIANS	203
X.	THE EPISTLE TO PHILEMON	228
XI.	THE EPISTLE TO THE EPHESIANS	249

THE EPISTLES
(FIRST SECTION

I.

INTRODUCTORY.

THE Gospel, which was founded by deeds, is spread by NARRATIVE. Narrative, not yet written, but current in the mouths of eye-witnesses and of holy men. The journal of that diffusion runs thus: 'Such an one went down to the city of such a people, and proclaimed unto them THE WORD. And the Word was concerning Jesus of Nazareth: how that God anointed Him with the Holy Ghost and with power: concerning his life, and his words, and his death, and his rising again, and his going up into heaven.' 'I received of the Lord that which also I delivered unto you,' writes St. Paul to the Corinthians, speaking of the great facts of the Resurrection. And it is to be observed that, in what follows, he enumerates the many separate appearances of the Lord in order, and calls to their mind how that he had given them all these details while he was among them. This points to a care and precision as regards the completeness and order of facts, which we should hardly have been disposed to predicate of the fervid Apostle of the Gentiles. And it is most valuable, as pointing to the kind of foundation which was laid before the Gospel testimony was committed to writing.

Perhaps we do not sufficiently realise in our imaginations the state of the newly founded Churches during this first and deeply interesting period. And perhaps in consequence we do not appreciate the full significance of the apostolic Epistles, and their entire appropriateness to the work which was then to be done.

Let us, by way of introduction to the Epistles, take the case of one such church, in Asia Minor or on the opposite shores of Greece, and endeavour to enter into its state and its wants.

Imagine a fair plain, with sheltering mountains. The scenery differs not much from that which some of us have seen in the south of Italy, save that the palm has somewhat encroached on the cypress and the olive: which latter trees however are found prevalent, and in luxuriance. The plain is bestridden with the arches of aqueducts, which have for their centre a fair group of buildings, whose columns are marked out by the fierce Eastern sun into lines of bright and dark alternating. That is the Acropolis—the temple fortress—the abode of the tutelar deities, whose images may be seen glittering in the sun, as we see to this day the saints on St. John Lateran glittering miles off over the Campagna at Rome. We are in a heathen land.

But let me enter the city: let me deliver my Christian note of introduction. The scene is very strange to me. Amidst a crowd of loungers, half-clad slaves, and children wholly naked, moves the heathen procession, with its ox adorned with garlands, and its sacrificing priest, girt at the waist, and his axe on his shoulder. It is plain who is in possession. But where is the little seed out of which shall grow the great tree, whose roots shall thrust out the plant that now fills the land? I deliver my letter: I enter into converse. What do I find?

A few months before, a holy man has taken his departure. He had been with them some weeks—

golden weeks — weeks of blessedness to their furthest memory. It had been an angel's visit. They take me up the Acropolis; there he stood and prayed: there he told them this or that Christian truth: the very cornices of the temple, the very coincident points in the look-out over land and distant sea, are full of the good tidings which he brought. They walk with me under the bright green of the caroubas, and the heavy shade of the ilexes, by which the paved road enters their city: there he walked up and down, and strengthened and comforted them: there first two or three of them who had visited Judæa, and seen that Countenance which none could forget, and heard Him speak like whom none else ever spoke, went forth on that memorable day to meet him—and here, under this Spina Christi, first fell his 'Salaam,' or 'Eirené,' or 'Pax vobiscum' on their ears. And by that other road, across whose long line of cypresses the mountain now casts its purple shadow, went he forth but the other day—all the gathered band with him: there, where we see the road rise bright over the knoll, he knelt and prayed: there they clasped their arms round him, and mingled their tears with his: there they stood and watched his little company lessen and vanish in the distance: and thence they returned home, sad indeed for a moment, but with a glorious hope full of immortality and joy.

But I re-enter the city with them, and in the shade of evening, and again under the moist dawn, I resort to their humble room of worship. Here is the centre and focus of the light which has been poured upon them. Here, from day to day, the holy man poured out his treasury of golden words —doubly precious now that the tone of his voice has departed. All that they know of the Son of God sounded from that spot, where he has stood far into the night, telling his wondrous story. There, too, he broke the bread, having told how the Lord did the same : thence he gave the Body broken, and dispensed the Blood shed, to the eye and the taste of Faith. All this remains vividly depicted on the memory. Joy and affection will not let them forget it. Nay, the Apostle, before he went, on a solemn day of the weekly festival of the Lord's Resurrection, laid his hands, and the hands of them that were with him, with prayer and fasting, on the heads of some among themselves ; and they keep up now that which he had begun, and repeat that which he had delivered to them.

So far, all is well. But, as I said, some months have gone by. Man cannot live wholly on the past. Unless there be knit up a link between the past and the present, unless in some form we can look on the past as present, the past will fade, and fade, and fade: and the importunate present will by degrees take its place. And this, in spite of all helps of other kinds than the one mentioned. The living voice is not enough, if it have only the past to speak of. That which meets the ear, has no permanent record. There is no *simultaneity* in sounds; as one enters, another departs. In course of time it may become even a question, what the first teacher delivered: some may report him one way, some another. The great oral tradition of the Gospel narrative, in its various forms, needed at length to be written down in order to gain permanence: how much more the teachings and inferences of any single messenger of the good tidings. But who could be trusted to do this? From the first, two great parties prevailed in almost every infant Christian community. The one, mainly composed of those believers who had been

Jews, would be likely to put into the recorded words more than they would fairly bear of the Judaistic spirit. With them, every saying which asserted the justice and holiness of the law would be taken as enforcing its observance on Christians. The other, the Gentile party, would be liable to report wrongly in the other direction, that of setting aside all the previous dispensation with its types and preparations for Christ, and perhaps also with some of those its moral sanctions and prohibitions, which are of eternal obligation, not because there enacted, but because they form portions of God's revelation of His eternal truth and justice. To these two parties might sometimes be added a third, that of the learned or philosophers, who were for effecting a compromise between Jewish cabalism and Gentile philosophy, and making the words reported to subserve such a purpose.

In the face of these difficulties, the apostolic teachers were directed to the expedient of writing letters to the churches which they had founded, or which owed their existence to emissaries sent from themselves. And surely no plan could have been more effectual, whether for the present emergency, or for future profit to the church. The questions which would need determining would be just those which were likely to recur again and again during the spread of the Gospel, and during the progress of individual churches. The relations of Christianity to social life and to heathen practices, —the observance of days and the abstinence from meats,—and other doubts arising from circumstances, would furnish examples of the application of the commands and maxims of Christ, and would call up the mention of first principles in a way which, when once exemplified, it might be easy to continue. And such letters would naturally also be employed in taking notice of any points in the conduct of those addressed which required correction, and thus would be led to dilate upon the great requirements of Christian morality. And where the writer was conscious of certain doctrines having been but insufficiently explained, he would naturally enlarge upon them; and would establish and enforce the belief of such as were likely to be called in question.

This would be the ordinary description of the purely occasional Epistle, written to a church after short absence, to impress the lessons given during the missionary visit.

To those who take a fair survey of the apostolic work, it will I think appear, that Epistles of this first kind must have been very numerous. Four such alone remain to us: two to the Corinthians and two to the Thessalonians; not taking into the number those written to individuals, which are better reckoned under another head. But, considering that St. Paul preached the Gospel from Jerusalem round about unto Illyricum, and that his fervid spirit carried in its sympathies all the churches, it can hardly be but that he must have sent Epistle upon Epistle, now lost to us, to churches of which perhaps we know not even the names. Two such Epistles are mentioned in his extant writings: one to Corinth (1 Cor. v.), and one to Laodicea (Col. iv.). One such is expressly asserted to have been written by St. John (3 John, ver. 9). It will hardly be credited that the idea, of any writings of Apostles being lost, has been by some, even in our own time, strongly objected to, on the ground that such writings would be inspired, and therefore cannot have been suffered to perish. The frivolity of this superstitious idea will at once be seen, if for 'writings' we substitute 'words.' Were not the words of the Apostles equally under the guidance of the Spirit who spoke within them? Would not they have been equally profitable to the Church in all ages? And yet where are the words of Paul at Antioch in Pisidia, the sum of which was that through much tribulation we must enter the kingdom of God? Where are the words with which he exhorted the assembly at Troas, when he continued his speech until midnight? This is the way in which the human probabilities in the course of the first preachers of Christianity have been lost in artificial theories, and their work divested of the reality and expansiveness of life.

Assuming then that a number of these occasional Epistles once existed, and judging of their contents by those which are left to us, we can easily imagine how the personal influence and the teaching of the Apostles were perpetuated by such reminders. This will be evident more in detail, when we come to consider the four Epistles which have been mentioned.

The convenience of the epistolary form of communication between the teacher and the taught would naturally give rise to the adoption of other forms of Epistles besides the occasional. The general, or *encyclical* Epistle, was made use of as a means of explaining and inculcating some special setting forth of the truth, and of warning against prevalent forms of error. Of this general Epistle we have examples from James the Lord's brother, from John the son of Zebedee, from Peter, and from Jude the brother of James. One remarkable Epistle of St. Paul—that to the Ephesians—seems, although addressed to a particular church, to partake of this catholic character: and under this head also must be set down the Epistle to the Hebrews, concerning which Origen, in the third century, could say, 'Who wrote it, God knoweth.' And we must not forget that, in its form, the Book of Revelation forms another such Epistle, addressed by the beloved Apostle, John the son of Zebedee, to the seven churches of Asia.

In proportion as these epistles are general, they depart from the true form of letters, and become more of pastoral allocutions or charges. Certain of these 'catholic' epistles appear to have at once assumed a position of authority as part of the Christian Scriptures. This may be inferred from their position in all the ancient copies of the New Testament; which is, next to the Acts of the Apostles, before the Epistles of St. Paul. In this number are comprehended the two of St. Peter (sometimes the first only, on which circumstance more will be said in another chapter), the three of St. John (though the second and third have no claim to the title 'general' or 'catholic'), and that of St. Jude. Next to these come the Epistles of St. Paul, no exceptional place being given to the Epistle to the Ephesians; and the Epistle to the Hebrews next before the Revelation; which last, in the ancient as in the modern copies, always closed the sacred canon.

There are yet some other kinds of epistles to be mentioned, neither occasional, nor general. From his prison in Rome the great Apostle of the Gentiles yearned for communion with those 'among whom he had gone, preaching the gospel of God.' And in this desire were included also others whom he had intended to visit, but had been prevented, 'who had not seen his face in the flesh.' We owe to this the Epistle to the Philippians and that to the Colossians. The latter of these was sent at the same time with the Epistle to the Ephesians, and probably during its writing had given rise to that more systematic exposition of the doctrine of the Christian Church. The Epistle to the Philippians was an outpouring of the Apostle's love towards a church of his peculiar affection, at a time when his own heart was full of sorrow, and his death seemed to be approaching.

Two of the greatest of St. Paul's Epistles have not yet been mentioned: the letter to the churches of Galatia, and that addressed to the congregation of Christians in the Metropolis of the world. Between these two there appears to be so intimate a relation that it is most natural to believe them to have been written at, or near about, the same time. And on examination it seems probable, as in the case of the two other Epistles, before mentioned, that the writing of the pointed and occasional letter gave rise in the Apostle's mind to the design of elaborating the more complete and systematic one. To the Galatians he wrote as their father in the faith, from whom they were rapidly seceding; to the Romans, who had never seen him in the imperial city, he wrote as the appointed Apostle of the Gentiles, hoping (as indeed proved to be the case) that his bodily presence among them might follow his pastoral treatise and exhortations.

The providence of God has not disdained to preserve, among the Christian canonical Scriptures, letters addressed to individuals. Of these, six have come down to us: four from the pen of St. Paul. The two to Timothy, and one to Titus, are precious to the Church in all ages, from being written on the subject of the choice, and duties, of the Christian ministry. The other, addressed to a private friend, Philemon, concerns a domestic matter, and exhibits to us a beautiful and graceful specimen of the interweaving of Christian feeling and sympathy with the incidents of common life. The other two are from the pen of St. John: the one, most probably, to a Christian lady, otherwise unknown: the other to a certain Gaius. Both are hortatory and general in their character: the latter, however, bringing before us various incidents and persons.

This enumeration of Epistles properly so called, should close with the most mysterious, and, in one respect, the most remarkable of all: that addressed to the Hebrews. The uncertainty of its authorship has been before mentioned. The lateness of its date is evident, from the allusions regarding present circumstances, and the statement which it contains of the handing down of the Gospel history from its eye-witnesses to the then living generation.

One part, however, of the promised testimony of the Comforter to the Church was yet in great part wanting. He was not only to bring to remembrance all that Christ himself had taught (John xiv. 26, xv. 26)—not only to enable the Apostles and apostolic men themselves to bear testimony (John xv. 27), and to guide them into all the truth (*ib.*), but he was finally *to show them things to come* (*ib.*). And therefore the New Testament canon closes with that great prophetic testimony of the Spirit of Jesus, received by the beloved Apostle in Patmos, and addressed by him in the form of an Epistle to the churches of his own especial jurisdiction in pro-consular Asia.

Thus we have the epistolary canon complete. We have been hitherto speaking of its various members formally, with reference to their occasion and constitution: let us now regard the whole with reference to its contents,—and to the question, What has the Church gained by its possession?

First, What is to be expected? Proceeding, as of course we must proceed, on the hypothesis of Christian belief, here we have the writings of men under a special outpouring of the Holy Spirit, an outpouring such as has never since been witnessed.

We believe these writings to have been intended for what they have since proved, the doctrinal charter of the future Christian Church. Nothing could be less like a *system*, than the teaching of our Blessed Lord. In these Epistles, the true comments on that teaching, we may expect great steps to be taken towards systematising it. The Lord's moral precepts, the Lord's mediatorial acts, are the seeds out of which, under his own direction, by his informing Spirit, the teaching of the Apostolic Epistles has grown. It is easy for any ignorant fellow to present to us a seed and a full-grown plant, and to argue, from their utter unlikeness, that the one is no development of the other. And just in this way has the comparison been made, by some calling themselves critics, between our Lord's teaching and the Epistles of his Apostles. As far as I have been able to study their arguments, they seem to me to amount to this: Were it not for St. Paul, St. Peter, St. John, St. James, St. Jude, and the Writer to the Hebrews, we never could have built up, out of our Lord's words and deeds, that system of theology which their Epistles enounce. To which I answer: Possibly not: certainly not, unless we were informed by the

Spirit which informed them. The educing from the Gospels, and from those further sayings of the Lord which the writers of these Epistles had heard, of the great doctrines of our faith, was a special work of God's Spirit, not the mere achievement of human logic. The process involved, as it went on, fresh revelations, in the unfolding of the Divine scheme of human salvation. Still, these revelations were in aid, not in suppression, of the common reason of mankind. They issued, not in the contradiction, but in the exposition, of our Lord's words and acts.

When then I find the Apostles arguing systematically for certain great doctrines as inferences from the facts of the Gospel, I find exactly that for which I am prepared: exactly that forward step which it was natural that God's providence should allow, and cause, next to be taken.

This being so, what has the Church gained by this addition of the Canon of Epistles to her historical sacred records?

I answer—First, the clear setting forth of the following great doctrines:—

1. The unity of three Divine Persons in the Godhead.

2. The person and office of the Son of God, incarnate in the flesh of man.

3. The inclusion and equality of all mankind in Him as its second and righteous Head.

4. The constitution in Him of a body, the Church, united to Him outwardly and visibly by sacramental ordinances, and inwardly and spiritually by faith and obedience.

5. As regards the outward and visible—the prescription, by divine command, or by inference, of these sacramental ordinances, symbolizing respectively the birth into, and the sustentation of, the new life of man's spirit,—and of an order of men to minister in sacred things.

6. As regards the inward and spiritual,—the effectual entrance of the individual soul by faith into the state of pardon and acceptance, and the progressive sanctification of man by the inhabitation and teaching of the Holy Spirit. Next,

7. The expansion and grounding of the doctrine of the Resurrection of the body, and its supplementing by various revelations concerning the last things.

8. Very numerous directions, too long to specify, concerning uncertain and difficult points of Chris-

tian practice in life: some, belonging of themselves to all ages of the Church: others, formally belonging to the times then present, but by analogy reflecting light upon corresponding difficulties in subsequent ages.

9. Warnings against error of different kinds, sometimes pointedly and antagonistically, sometimes conveyed in strenuous and detailed upholding of the corresponding dogmatic truth: thus furnishing an armoury, offensive and defensive, for the Church in all ages.

10. The concluding portion of the New Testament has also dowered the Church with a rich treasure of prophetic encouragement and warning, mysterious indeed, and awaiting future explanation in detail, but in its general scope and tendency of undoubted application: all pointing on to the second Advent of the Lord, and keeping the Church in an attitude of expectation of His appearing.

11. We may add to these particulars, the precious examples of the holy men who wrote the Epistles,— of which no page is destitute. No formal treatises could ever have had the effect of such letters, admitting us into the very life and heart of the writer The Epistles of St. Paul, said by Luther to be 'not

dead words, but living creatures with hands and feet,' edify and comfort the Church not only by the doctrines which they establish, not only by the direct words of consolation with which they abound, but also, and perhaps on the whole, principally, by the spectacle which they present to us of a man penetrated with the spirit of holiness, steeped in the love of Christ, living his life in the flesh by the faith of the Son of God : undergoing almost superhuman afflictions and toils in the midst of bodily infirmity and mental depression; with a thorn in his flesh, which is not removed, because Christ's grace is sufficient for him.

In these matters the holy Apostles are the intensified pictures of ourselves : their little words and seemingly trivial remarks gain unexpected weight when the perplexed soul holds the balances of hope and fear, of desire and repugnance : their obscurest sayings leap out into sudden light, when the spirit is walking in dark valleys, where the Father's countenance is hidden.

12. The last use of the epistolary canon which I shall mention is, that of furnishing running comments on various points of the apostolical history as narrated in the Acts of the Apostles. As I write

this, I am quite aware that persons have in our own time been found, who deny that any such correspondence exists, as will make the Epistles confirm the history. I have read some of the arguments by which they seek to establish their hostile position. But it has ever seemed to me that common sense is all for the received Christian view, while the praise of ingenious subtlety, if worth having, may be fairly conceded to the impugners of that view. Take the arguments of Paley's 'Horæ Paulinæ,' and you may apply them to any sober piece of similar evidence in common life: they are the considerations by which we are convinced, and upon which we act, day by day. But take example from *their* arguments,—proceed in their way of attack, and you may thus in a few minutes demolish any plain matter of historical fact. This has been shown over and over again: by Whately, for example, in his 'Historic Doubts respecting Napoleon Bonaparte,' and by an ingenious American, cited in an article in the *Quarterly Review* for last October, who proved, on Strauss's method, that the Declaration of Independence was never signed. Such weapons may be convenient for partisans, but do not suit fair-dealing people. We do not approve of the poacher's night-hooks and springes, however much game they may succeed in destroying. We look with abhorrence on an enemy who poisons wells and fountains. Give us the weapons of fair and honest men, and we are not afraid of the battle.

In my next paper I hope to begin at once to deal with the Epistles separately. My plan will be to proceed with them, as far as I am able, in chronological order. That adopted in the common arrangement of the canon has been chosen without reference to chronology. It proceeds apparently on consideration of the relative length and importance of the Epistles, giving, however, to St. Paul the preference. After his thirteen was placed the Epistle to the Hebrews, as being, if not by him, an appendix by some hand almost guided by his. Then followed the 'catholic' Epistles—then the Revelation.

This plan has the advantage of something like system, and is, perhaps, for convenience of reference, the best. But our purpose is a different one. It is, to set before the reader the circumstances under which each Epistle was written, and to try to bring about an intelligent view of the purpose and character of each. The chronological order thus becomes for us inevitable. The missionary journey last preceding: the character of the Apostle's visit among the people addressed, and its incidents, will be most important for us: and if we had to notice these, taking the Epistles in their present existing order, we should have continually to be going back and going forward, and breaking up the continuity of the apostolic progress.

Giving, therefore, the first place to St. Paul, we shall proceed regularly through his Epistles. The first which will thus come before us in order will be the Letters written to the Church of the Thessalonians.

That portion of each article which takes note of erroneous and inadequate renderings in our Authorised English Version, will, in the treatment of the Epistles, assume much more importance than before. In fact, it will be very difficult to prevent it from extending beyond reasonable limits. In some of the Epistles, especially in their argumentative portions, the inferential connection is so disguised in our version, that nothing less than a recast of the whole sentence will at all represent the true meaning.

So that, while the reader's pardon will sometimes have to be asked for, and his patience will be somewhat largely taxed, we must make up our minds to incur, as we have done before, grave reprehension at the hands of those who are for keeping the Authorised Version at all hazards; who think it safer to abide by the gloss of man, than to search into the mind of God.

THE FIRST EPISTLE TO THE THESSALONIANS.

FIRST, who were the Thessalonians? And how came St. Paul among them? If you turn to Acts xvi., you will find the account of his 'shameful treatment' and honourable dismissal 'at Philippi.' Then, in chap. xvii. 1, we read that, 'having passed through Amphipolis and Apollonia, they (Paul and Silas and Timothy) came to Thessalonica.' The former of these two, Amphipolis, is a mass of ruins: even the site of the latter is not known. But Thessalonica was then, ever has been, and is now, under the slightly abridged name of Saloniki, a great and flourishing city. The Apostle and his companions travelled to it through a beautiful country of lakes, streams, and mountains. The outlet of a ravine which they had been climbing gave to their sight wide plains and the blue Ægean; and over the edge of the slope which was between them and the sea, were visible the walls and towers of Thessalonica, itself built on the descent right down to the water's edge.

In the last town in which the Apostle had preached, the Jews were content with a mere place of prayer by the river side. But here there was a (or rather *the*) synagogue of the Jews. They dwelt at Thessalonica in great numbers, and have continued to do so all through the ages which have since passed. We are told that their number is now 35,000, half the entire population: that they have 36 synagogues: that the greater part of the trade of the place is in their hands.* I may remark to the reader, by the way, that this permanence and prosperity of the Thessalonian Jews may teach him a lesson, not to be too hasty in pronouncing the opposite features in a people's history to be a judgment from God. No Jews treated St. Paul worse than these: none have been more uniformly populous and prosperous.

* See Conybeare and Howson's 'Life of St. Paul,' to which work I owe many of the details of which my descriptions are made up.

But the Apostle and his companions enter the city. Whether they were at once lodged in the house of Jason, where we afterwards find them, does not appear certain. Whether there were believers in Thessalonica before the Apostle's arrival, we are not informed. We know that, while he was in the city, he laboured night and day for his own subsistence. (1 Thess. ii. 9.) Possibly he may have joined some company of workmen in the Cilician hair-cloth, the making of which was his trade. His exceeding unwillingness to be chargeable to any of them looks rather as if he were not at first any one's guest, but lodging somewhere on his own account. At once (he appears to have come late in the week) he sought the synagogue of the Jews. At once he opened his message regarding Christ. Three Sabbath-days his preaching was continued. And, doubtless, he was not idle during the week; for in his description (1 Thess. i. 9) of his preaching and its results, he reminds the Thessalonians how they 'turned from idols to serve the living God,' which could only be said of Gentiles, who would not be likely to be present in the synagogue. We have a very full description of the way in which the Gospel was announced by him. He spoke simply and plainly: not flattering the rich and busy city, but speaking his message 'with much contention,' 'not as pleasing men, but God which trieth the hearts.' And the reception which his message met with was remarkable. They received it, not as the word of men, but as the word of God. They who heard it formed themselves into a church, in which, though there were doubtless many Jews, yet beyond question the preponderance was on the side of the Gentiles. It has been observed that in neither of these Epistles is there so much as one allusion to the Old Testament Scriptures: a significant fact, when we remember how steeped St. Paul's mind was in all their lore. This does not look as if the readers were to be mainly Jews. Some however of the Jews became believers, and attached themselves to Paul and Silas (Acts xvii. 4). But the great body of believers was composed of Greek proselytes: and to these were added, as indeed seems to have been the case everywhere else, many of the chief women of the city.

For upwards of three weeks the influence of the Apostle was on the increase. Each Sabbath-day, we may well imagine, he entered further into the nature of the "good tidings," and opened and alleged new reasons why Christ must needs have suffered and risen again from the dead; and why this Jesus whom he preached to them was to be received as Christ.

Such a course could not but stir up the hostility of those Jews who rejected the message. As usual, where argument was wanting, violence was resorted to. They gathered together the rabble of the market, collected a multitude, and rioted in the streets; directing their attack upon the house of Jason, with whom apparently the missionaries were lodging. Not finding them, they laid hold on the householder himself, and some of the believers whom they took there, and brought them before the magistrates.

And here let us pause a moment to notice a feature of genuine truth in the narrative. These magistrates of Thessalonica are called by an unusual name: viz., *Politarchs*, or *rulers of the citizens*. First of all, we might well suppose that some peculiar name would be used at Thessalonica; for it was what we called a 'free city,' *i.e.*, not like Philippi, a *colony*, governed after the manner of Rome itself, a little miniature of the metropolis, but a town left to its own government and customs. So that, if the magistrates were called by some strange title, we might suppose that it was owing to local custom which had not been interfered with. So far we should be justified in believing that St. Luke had been faithful in his report, and we might conclude, from this incidental notice of the name, that it was in use at Thessalonica. That is, the believer in the Scripture narrative would give him this credit: the unbeliever would probably find in the name an occasion for denying the accuracy of the narrative. However, we have not been left in this case to mere inference. An inscription exists to this day on a triumphal arch at Thessalonica, stating that it was erected *while Sosipater, Secundus, Gaius, and others were politarchs.* It will be also observed that the three names which I have selected out of the list belong also to three of St. Paul's companions in travel; for Sosipater is only a longer form of Sopater (Acts xx. 4), who was of the neighbouring city of Berœa; and Gaius was of Macedonia (Acts xix. 29), Secundus of Thessalonica itself (Acts xx. 4). So accurate does research ever prove the Scripture narrative to have been. The reader is not indeed to imagine that the bearers of these names, as recorded on the arch, were *identical* with St. Paul's companions. The arch itself is probably of the age of the Emperor Constantine—250 years later. But the inscription proves that the magistrates were called by the very name which St. Luke gives them; and that the names of St. Paul's Macedonian companions were of current use in that neighbourhood.

The immediate result of the appearance of Jason and his friends was to excite and harass the politarchs. The Apostle was charged with disloyalty to Cæsar, and with 'saying that some one else was king, even Jesus;' an awkward charge for a free city under the Roman empire to deal with. Not willing to commit themselves to a decision, the magistrates contented themselves with binding over Jason and his friends to keep the public peace.

Both for this reason and on account of the hostility of the Jews, Thessalonica was no longer a place for the Christian missionaries; and accordingly they were privately conveyed away by night to Berœa. Such is the brief history of St. Paul's visit to this city; about a month, more or less, was its duration: and it gave occasion to the two remarkable letters which we find in our Testaments. Let us now see how this was.

The charge brought against the preachers by the Jews is very instructive on this head. It is plain that the headship and the kingdom of Christ had been a main subject of their discourses. The rough and unjust treatment of St. Paul at Philippi had roused his spirit, so that he boldly and freely proclaimed the good news of a coming reign of one who should judge the world in righteousness, trying the hearts of men (1 Thess. ii. 2). We find traces of this preaching of the kingdom and coming of the Lord in both the letters. Thus, for instance, in 1 Thess. i. 10, their conversion is described as having resulted in their serving the living and true God, and *waiting for His Son from the heavens;* and in the same (ii. 12) they are exhorted to walk worthy of the God who calleth them to *His kingdom and glory.* See also chap. ii. 19, 20; iii. 13; iv. 13—18; v. 1—11, and 23. The most remarkable of all these passages (iv. 13—18) appears to have been written in reply to a fear of the Thessalonians, lest their friends who had fallen asleep in Christ should be excluded from the triumph and glory of His second coming. That they had misunderstood the Apostle's words, is plain from his remonstrance with them in the second Epistle (ii. 5) where, having set forth to them the things which must happen before the coming of the Lord, he says, 'Do ye not remember that while I was yet with you, I was in the habit of telling you these things?' Their enthusiasm had outrun even the Apostle's plain speaking; they regarded the day of the Lord as actually upon them, and its glories as something which would be missed by those who died before the Lord himself should appear. As far as we can gather, there appear to have been two distinct phases of their misapprehension: the first, concerning their deceased friends; then, when that had been removed by a plain declaration that when Christ should come they would accompany Him, another mistake as to the immediate coming of the day itself, which it is St. Paul's aim to correct in the second Epistle.

But we must now pass from notices of the message at first delivered, to the circumstances under which the two Epistles were written.

The Gospel at first made prosperous way at Beroea: but from that city again the missionaries were driven out by the malice of the Thessalonian

Jews, who came and raised a tumult there also. On this, the principal member of the mission, and the most obnoxious to the Jews, was sent away alone by the brethren: it would appear, with secret orders in the route to elude the vigilance of the enemy.

It is not our object now to dwell on the memorable visit of St. Paul to Athens. We accompany him thence to Corinth, where we have a notice (Acts xviii. 5) of his companions, Silas and Timothy, having rejoined him from Macedonia. It would appear, from comparing Acts xvii. 15 with 1 Thess. iii. 2, that he had sent back by those brethren, who conducted him to Athens, a message to Timothy (and Silas) to visit the Thessalonian church, to establish them, and exhort them concerning their faith, and then to rejoin him as quickly as possible. The nature of the report brought him by his companions sufficiently appears in the first letter. It had been, on the whole, most favourable. The word of the Lord (*i.e.*, concerning Christ) had sounded abroad from them, not only in their own country but everywhere: they were cause of great joy to their father in the faith. But there appear to have been some blemishes. There was a tendency to adopt or fall back into the immoral habits of the heathen world: there was some want of brotherly love and quiet earnestness, and a disposition to meddle and to be indolent: and there was the great mistake to which we have before made allusion, respecting those who had fallen asleep in Christ.

Under these circumstances the first letter was written. When the tidings from Macedonia arrived, they found the Apostle in an anxious and trying state. He was, we are told, constrained in spirit, testifying to the Jews that Jesus was the Christ. It was the same kind of work in which he had had such conflict at Thessalonica, and the message brought up before him again all the fervour and love with which his preaching, though strongly opposed, had been there received. He employed his scanty intervals of retirement in pouring out his heart to his beloved Thessalonians. It was apparently the first time that the Divine Spirit had prompted him to preach the Gospel in writing. Of course we cannot be certain of this, because some of his Epistles have been lost; but at all events this is the first of his letters that has come down to us, and it is interesting in that light, as well as on all other accounts. We see from it what was the natural course of his feelings towards those among whom he had preached with success. We see how large a portion of his heart was given to love and gratitude, how rejoiced he was to praise and encourage, how unwilling to blame. There is no Epistle that shows us the spontaneous out-flowing of the Apostle's mind to his converts so plainly as this. And it is all the more interesting, as also making it evident how the unfolding of the great doctrinal system of Christian truth was, even with the Apostles themselves, a gradual thing. In these earlier Epistles there is nothing of that deep dogmatic teaching which becomes so prevalent as time goes on, and almost pervades the later Epistles written during the Roman captivity: here all is affectionate remembrance, and fresh, fervid exhortation, grounded on the elementary facts and hopes of the Gospel. I have said elsewhere,* 'The earliest of the Epistles are ever moral and practical, the advanced ones more doctrinal and spiritual. It was not till it appeared that the bulwark of salvation by grace must be strengthened, that the

---

* "New Testament for English Readers," Introduction, ch. viii. § 4, ar. 3.

building on the one foundation must be raised thus impregnable to the righteousness of works and the law, that the Epistles to the Galatians and the Romans were given through the great Apostle, reaching to the full breadth and height of the great argument. Then followed the Epistles of the imprisonment, building up higher and higher the edifice there consolidated; and the Pastoral Epistles, suited to a more developed ecclesiastical condition, and aimed at the correction of abuses which sprung up later, or were the ripened fruit of former doctrinal errors.'

It is remarkable that the one point as to which experience brought to the Apostle the greatest 'desire to change his voice,' was that very one which our Lord in solemn terms had left in uncertainty for all ages of his militant Church—even the day of the second coming. His teaching at Thessalonica had indeed been misunderstood. He himself protests against the sense which had been put upon it. But even misunderstanding points to some tendency in the direction which it has taken. St. Paul's manner of dwelling on and describing the day of the Lord, without perhaps putting in the cautions which he afterwards gave against the idea that it was immediately at hand, had been interpreted as pointing to a very short interval before it should be upon them. 'We which are alive and remain' may represent a class of similar expressions not thus meant by the speaker, but capable of conveying the idea that the hearers should see the Lord's appearing in their own time. I again quote from the same Introduction as before: 'The time of our Lord's coming was hidden from all created beings,—nay, in the mystery of his mediatorial office, from the Son himself (Mark xiii. 32). Even after His Resurrection, when questioned by the Apostles as to the time of his restoring the kingdom of Israel, His reply is still, that it is not for them to know the times and the seasons, which the Father hath put in his own power (Acts i. 7).' Here then is a plain indication, which has not, I think, been sufficiently made use of in judging of the Epistles. The Spirit was to *testify of Christ:* to take of the things of Christ and show them unto the Apostles. So that, however much that Spirit, in His infinite wisdom, might be pleased to impart to them of the details and accompanying circumstances of the Lord's appearing, we may be sure that the truth spoken by our Lord, 'Of that day and hour knoweth no man,' would hold good with regard to them, and be traced in their writings. If they were true men, and their words and epistles the genuine production of inspiration of them by that Spirit of Truth, we may expect to find in such speeches and writings tokens of their appointed uncertainty of the day and hour; expectations, true in expression and fully justified by appearance, yet corrected, as God's purposes were manifested, by advancing experience and larger effusions of the spirit of prophecy. If then I find in the course of St. Paul's Epistles, that expressions which occur in the earlier ones, and seem to indicate expectation of the Lord's almost immediate coming, are gradually modified,—disappear altogether in the Epistles of the imprisonment,—and are succeeded by others speaking in a very different strain, of 'dissolving, and being with Christ,' and passing through death and the resurrection, in the latest Epistles,—I regard it, not as a strange thing, not as a circumstance which I must explain away for fear of weakening the authority of his Epistles, but as exactly that which I should expect to find: as the very strongest testimony that these Epistles were written by one who was left in this uncertainty—not by one who wished to make it appear that inspiration had rendered him omniscient. And in this, the earliest of those Epistles, I do find exactly that which I might expect on this head. While every word and every detail respecting the Lord's coming is a perpetual inheritance for the Church,—while we continue to comfort one another with the glorious and heart-stirring sentences which he utters to us 'in the word of the Lord,' no candid eye can help seeing in the Epistle how the uncertainty of 'the day and hour' has tinged all these passages with a hue of near anticipation: how natural it was that the Thessalonians, receiving this Epistle, should have allowed that anticipation to be brought even yet nearer, and have imagined the day to have been actually at hand.

The nature of the contents of this first Epistle will have been already surmised. It was written because the Apostle wanted to fill up by exhortation and consolation the necessary defects of a teaching, which had been indeed most earnest and plain as far as it had gone, but had been broken off before it was complete. The earlier portion of the letter is spent in congratulating the Thessalonians and praising them for the simplicity and readiness with which they had received his message, and for the eminence of their faith, which had become since then matter of notoriety: in reminding them also of the whole character of his own demeanour among them: his disinterested independence of them, and gentle, even mother-like, affection towards them. He next recalls to mind the hostility of the Jews, not so much to himself as to them, and draws a comparison between them and the churches of Judea in this respect (14—16). Then he touches gently his own case, showing how this same hostility had, since his departure, defeated one and another scheme which he had made for seeing them (17—20). The third chapter is occupied with a narrative of the circumstances under which the report of Timothy respecting them had reached him, and with expressions of thankfulness and affection resulting thereupon; concluding (11—13) with a wish for the possibility of his visiting them, and for their increase in love and holiness, that they might be blameless before God at the Lord's coming. And only now begin the practical exhortations and corrections of defects. These correspond to the order in which those defects have been noted above. Thessalonica seems, like its wealthy sister Corinth, to have been disgraced by the prevalent practice of immorality. The disciples there are, in consequence, exhorted to purity, and to the chaste adoption of that only method which God has provided for man's lawful use. Next he very gently touches on a want of brotherly love, blaming, where he seems to praise, as was often his habit. And thus he passes on to that which is in the mind of every Christian, *the great passage* in the Epistle: the revelation respecting the state and prospects of the dead in Christ. I have before spoken of the mistake which they had made; let us now see how St. Paul corrects it.

They who had, through the victory of Jesus, exchanged death for sleep (see below), are gone to Jesus, and when God brings Him back to us, they will also be brought together with Him. For the order which shall be observed—no device of the Apostle's own mind, but revealed to him by the Lord—will be this: the living will have no advantage over the sleeping, because the Lord himself shall come down from heaven and awake the dead, who, before anything else is done, shall rise—their spirits, which came with Jesus, being united to their bodies which were sleeping; and, this being done, the living, who remain behind on earth, will be caught up into the air to meet the Lord [and them]. Thus were they to be comforted, and not to sorrow as if their dear friends had lost anything; for, in fact, they had been the gainers: and supposing that day to come in their own time, would have the advantage over *them*.

And now he goes on to speak of that great day itself, in terms which doubtless they in their eagerness fastened upon, and interpreted of its too speedy coming. Now occurs the first of those afterwards often-repeated exhortations to walk in light, as children of the day (see also Rom. xiii. 12, 13; Eph. v. 8; Col. i. 12, 13); now is found the first germ of that description of the armour of God, or of light, which he afterwards expanded so gloriously (Eph. vi. 10). Now also first we come to those short insulated admonitions which have been compared to strings of pearls,—with which in after years he was in the habit of coming towards the conclusion of his Epistles (see Rom. xii. 9—18; 1 Cor. xvi. 13, 14; 1 Tim. iv. 11—16; 2 Tim. iv. 1—5). We may remark that he concludes the Epistle in full consciousness of its inspired and authoritative character. 'I adjure you by the Lord,' he says, 'that this Epistle be read unto all the holy brethren.' Such vehemence would ill become the writer of any mere human letter. And this remark is important considering it is the earliest among his Epistles. He wrote in full consciousness of his apostolic power.

The second Epistle is far too important, as to the explanation of one portion of its contents, to be included in the remaining short space allotted to this chapter. We hope to devote our next to its consideration. Meantime we may make an observation on a matter which is especially worth notice in this earliest Epistle. Though the Apostle, in the address of both, associates with himself Silvanus (Silas) and Timothy, who had been his companions in preaching the Word at Thessalonica, and continues this method of speech by the use of the first person plural as far as ch. xi. 18, yet there he explains 'we' to mean, 'I, Paul,' and when he recurs to it again, asserts that which was true of himself alone and not of his two companions (ch. iii. 1). But he soon breaks away into the first person singular (ch. iii. 5), and though most of the remainder of the Epistle is expressed in the plural form, yet in his final adjuration he confines himself to the singular. This serves to shew, that, though more names than one may be mentioned at the beginning of an Epistle, and though the formality of using the plural prevail through the greater part of it, yet it is the apostolic authority of St. Paul himself which is the sanction of the whole, and the individual thought of St. Paul that works out the arguments and enforces the exhortation.

We now proceed to the recounting of the more important varieties in reading, and corrections in rendering, necessary to be noticed in this Epistle.

Of the former, there are but few, and these not of the first importance.

In ch. i. 1, some of our oldest authorities omit the words '*from God our Father and the Lord Jesus Christ.*' And though other authorities almost as ancient contain the words, the omission seems to point to the original text. *Elsewhere* the corresponding words are not omitted, and it is probable that they may have been inserted here to conform this to those other places.

In ch. ii. 19, '*Christ*' is omitted in all our oldest authorities, and should certainly be erased.

In ch. iii. 2, for 'and minister of God and our fellow labourer in the Gospel of Christ,' our ancient MSS. have very various expressions. The Vatican has only the words 'and fellow worker;' the Sinaitic and Alexandrine have only 'and minister of God;' the Claromontane MS. has 'and fellow-worker with God in the Gospel of Christ,' which is most likely to have been the original text, and to have been varied on account of the difficulty presented by the unusual expression. In verses 11 and 13, the word 'Christ' is omitted in all the most ancient MSS. 'The Lord Jesus' seems to have been at this time St. Paul's constant way of naming the Saviour. And it is to be noted, that he was charged at Thessalonica before the magistrates with proclaiming '*another king, one Jesus.*'

In ch. iv. 1, after the words 'please God,' all our most ancient MSS. insert 'even as also ye are walking.' In ver. 7, '*us*' should be read 'you.' In ver. 13 all our most ancient MSS., instead of 'I,' have 'we.'

In ch. v. 3, at the beginning, '*For*' is omitted by the Alexandrine and Sinaitic MSS., and in the ancient Syriac version and the most ancient Fathers: the Vatican and Claromontane MSS.

read 'But.' In ver. 5, all the oldest authorities begin the verse 'For ye are,' &c. In ver. 20, 21, the words ought to stand 'Despise not prophesyings, but prove all things;' *i.e.*, on the one hand do not think lightly of any utterances of the word of God by whomsoever made: on the other, do not be led by everything so spoken, but put all things to the test. See on this place below.

We now come to what will prove, in the Epistles, the far more serious task, that of enumerating passages in which our English version fails to give the force, and very often the correct meaning, of the original.

In ch. i. 3, '*hope in our Lord Jesus Christ*' is incorrect. The original has '*hope of our Lord Jesus Christ*,' *i.e.*, of his coming—the great subject of the Epistle. In ver. 4, '*knowing, brethren beloved, your election of God*,' should be, 'knowing, brethren beloved by God, your election.' In ver. 8, '*sounded*' should be 'hath sounded.' The Apostle is speaking, not of a thing long past, but of one which had just taken place, and was then continuing. In ver. 10, '*delivered*' ought to be 'delivereth.'

In ch. ii. 1, '*was not*' should be 'hath not

been.' In ver. 2, for '*was not*' should stand 'springeth not' or 'cometh not.' The Apostle is speaking, not of what his exhortation *was* when he was with them, but of its general character: compare 'Even so we *speak*' (not '*spoke*'), below. In ver. 4, '*were allowed*' should be 'have been approved.' In ver. 7 the expression '*even as a nurse cherisheth her children*' is open to mistake, besides being an insufficient rendering of the original words. It may be supposed that the 'nurse' is a mere hired servant, and the children hers, merely as entrusted to her. But the original has, as if a nurse should cherish HER OWN children: and the best way of conveying the meaning in English would be to render, 'like as when a nursing-mother cherisheth her own children.' In ver. 8, '*souls*' ought to be 'lives.' In ver. 10, '*among*' should be 'toward.'* In ver. 12, '*hath called*' should be 'calleth.' In ver. 14, '*followers*' is better rendered literally, 'imitators.' In ver. 15, '*have persecuted*' should be 'drove out.' In ver. 16, '*is come*' should be 'came.' The meaning is somewhat obscure,

* I may be allowed to mention, that in my "New Testament for English Readers" there is a misprint in the text of ver. ii. The words 'every one of you' should come after 'comforting you,' and not in their present position.

and therefore the original tense should be carefully kept. The present English version gives the impression that the destruction of Jerusalem had passed, whereas it did not happen till eighteen years after.

Ch. iii. 2, '*comfort*' should probably be 'exhort.' Ver. 13, '*God even our Father*,' should be 'God and our Father,' *i. e.*, 'Him who is our God and Father.'

Ch. iv. 1, '*by the Lord Jesus*' should be 'in the Lord Jesus,' *i. e.* literally as the original. The expression is not a form of adjuration, but sets forth the holy element in which his exhortation was made. In ch. v. 29, the expression is quite a different one. In the same verse '*have received*' ought to be 'received.' He means when he was with them and taught them. In ver. 4, '*how to possess his vessel*' is a mis-translation. It should be 'how to acquire his own vessel,' and it means, how to take a wife who might be his own lawful vessel for that purpose which the sin in question carried out unlawfully. In ver. 6 again, the sense is utterly confused by a mistake of our translators. By rendering '*in any matter*,' they have made it appear as if the sin of defrauding another, generally, were that against which the Apostle is warning: and thus the whole passage becomes incoherent, and loses its solemn force. The words which they have rendered '*in any matter*,' stand in the original 'in the matter,' *i. e.*, in this matter, which is now in hand, viz., the unclean lusts of the flesh. The Apostle is speaking in language somewhat veiled, for decency's sake. In the same verse, '*have* forewarned' should be 'forewarned;' and in the next verse, '*hath not called us*' should be 'calleth us not;' and the next should proceed, 'for uncleanness, but in sanctification.' In the next verse, '*who hath also given*' ought to be 'who also gave.' In ver. 13, for '*others*' should stand 'the rest.' In ver. 14, '*sleep in Jesus*' ought to be 'fell asleep through Jesus,' *i. e.*, by his merits have had their death turned into sleep. 'Sleep in Jesus' is a beautiful and true expression: but it is not the one used here. In the same verse, '*with him*' may be misunderstood. 'Him' does not refer to God, but to Jesus: will God bring, at the same time that He brings HIM, Jesus, through whom they fell asleep. It would be better, therefore, to express it, 'together with Him,' which can hardly be mistaken. In ver. 15, 'shall not prevent' would be much better expressed 'shall in no wise have the advantage of.' In ver. 17 it is necessary to notice that 'together' does not belong to 'with them:' it is not, 'shall be caught up, together with them, to meet the Lord,' but 'shall be caught up together, with them, to meet the Lord.' To make this plain, I have in my revised text inserted the word 'all:' 'shall be caught up all together, with them, to meet the Lord.'

Ch. v. 1: 'ye have no need *that I write unto you*' is literally 'ye have no need to be written unto.' The Authorised Version puts 'I' into too much prominence. It seems as if some one else might be thought of, who ought to write to them on this point. In ver. 5, '*the children*' ought to be 'sons' (twice). Ver. 6, '*others*' should be 'the rest.' Ver. 9, '*hath not* appointed us' should be 'appointed us not.' In ver. 10, 'together,' again, is not to be joined to 'with Him,' but it should be read, 'should live together, with Him.' In ver. 15, the words should stand, 'both toward one another, and toward all.' The preposition is the same in both clauses. Ver. 22 as it stands in our version is undoubtedly wrong, and has misled many persons, who have thought it to be an injunction to abstain even from that which *seems* evil,—to avoid all chance of offence. The words mean nothing of the kind, but merely this: 'Abstain from every form of evil,' *i. e.*, 'from every species,' 'every kind, of evil.' And they correspond with the former member of the sentence, which should be divided, further, by a comma only, 'Hold fast that which is good, abstain from every kind of evil.'

III.

THE SECOND EPISTLE TO THE THESSALONIANS.

TWO suppositions are possible with regard to the occasion of the Apostle's writing this second Epistle. The first is, that the Thessalonians had misunderstood what he had said in his former Epistle regarding the second coming of our Lord, and imagined that day to be close upon them. But to this there are two objections. First, that there is nothing in the former Epistle which could well have given rise to such an amount of misunderstanding. Had it been previously existing, or had it come upon them afterwards from some other influence, there might be nothing in that Epistle to check it: but we can hardly conceive it to have arisen from that letter alone. And secondly, St. Paul's own words in this Epistle hardly bear out such a supposition. The Thessalonians are cautioned not to be " shaken in mind nor troubled, neither by spirit (spiritual gift of prophecy), nor by word, nor by letter as by us.' This would look as if some Epistle had been circulated among them purporting to come, but not really coming, from their Father in the faith. And so Chrysostom takes the passage to mean: 'He seems to me here to hint, that some were going about with a forged Epistle pretending to be from Paul, and that showing this they affirmed the day of the Lord to be already come, that they might deceive many. And this supposition also derives confirmation from the care taken in ch. iii. 17, to add to this Epistle, itself written by an amanuensis, an autograph salutation, and to specify such autograph salutation to be the token of genuineness which the Apostle intended ever after to employ.' And more confirmation still is obtained for this view, from the circumstance that, if this second Epistle were intended for a correction of the first, it serves the purpose very insufficiently, opening in ch. i. 7, with an anticipation of Christ's coming quite as ardent and realising as any in that former Epistle.

We adopt then unhesitatingly the second hypothesis: that since the sending of that letter, some one had been imposing upon the Thessalonians a letter in the Apostle's name, to the effect that the day of the Lord was close upon them; exciting them, and causing them to walk disorderly, and to disregard their own business in life. On being informed of this at Corinth, where he remained for a year and a half, he sent this second Epistle, not contradicting, not even modifying, his former teaching, but filling it out and rendering it complete: informing them of those things which in the divine counsels were destined to precede the coming of the day of the Lord, and the manifestation of which was kept back by circumstances then existing. Unquestionably, this great prophetic passage is the glory, as it furnished the main object, of this second Epistle. It will be my endeavour, first to regard the Epistle as a whole, and then to give particular attention to the interpretation of this passage.

This Epistle is superscribed, as the former one was, by Paul and Silvanus (Silas) and Timothy. It would seem as if some little time must have elapsed since the former Epistle, enough both to have brought on the Thessalonians length of persecution sufficient for endurance under it to be predicated of them, and enough also to give rise to Christian churches in Corinth and its neighbourhood: for the Apostle speaks (ch. i. 4) of his 'boasting of them in the churches of God for their patience and faith in all their persecutions and afflictions that they were enduring.' This endurance is treated by him as a token of God's justice, preparing them for His kingdom, at the revelation of which they should have rest, and their persecutors recompense of affliction. The manifestation of that kingdom is spoken of in the same tone as prevailed in the former Epistle: thus making it manifest that it is not the intention of the Apostle to correct or change anything which he had before written to them. He now (ch. ii.) addresses himself to the great mistake under which they were labouring: and having both reminded them of his former teaching, and imparted to them again the great truths on the matter which he had then declared to them, he repeats his thankfulness for them, and exhorts them to hold fast the traditions which they have been taught, whether by word, or by his Epistles.

In drawing to a close, he begs their prayers for the success of his great work, and for his own deliverance from the Jews, then violently contending with him at Corinth: expressing his confidence in the Thessalonians, and praying for them in turn that their hearts may be led into the love of God, and the patience of which Christ was the example.

Then follow his final injunctions; and their character, as has been already hinted, shews beyond mistake what had been the effect of their mistake which he has been correcting. Some among them were walking disorderly, not working at any business, but being busy bodies: contrary both to the Apostle's teaching, and to his consistent example when he was among them. These persons he exhorts solemnly to return to their occupations, and in quietness to earn their own bread. From such as will not, he commands the believers to separate themselves; not, however, in a hostile spirit, but with brotherly admonitions. And then, having given them a sure token of the genuineness of this letter, *viz.*, the salutation written with his own hand, his token in every Epistle, he concludes with the valedictory prayer, that the favour of Christ might ever abide with them.

We now approach the consideration of the important passage in chapter ii. It may be well first to present it in English, as nearly as possible in a literal translation from the original.

'*But we beseech you, brethren, touching the coming of our Lord Jesus Christ, and our gathering together unto Him, that ye be not soon shaken from your mind, nor yet be troubled, neither by spirit nor by word, nor by letter as if by us* [*i. e.*, with pretence of our authority], *to the effect that the day of the Lord is come. Let no man deceive you in any way: for* ['*that day shall not come,*' or '*it shall not be so.*' nothing answering to these words is expressed in the original] *unless there shall have come the apostasy first, and the man of sin* [our two most ancient MSS. have '*of lawlessness*'] *shall have been revealed, the son of perdition; he that opposeth, and exalteth himself above every one called God, or an object of worship: so that he sitteth down in the temple of God, showing himself that he is God. Remember ye not that when I was yet with you, I used to tell you these things? And now ye know what hindereth, that he may be revealed in his own time. For the mystery of lawlessness doth already work, only until he that now hindereth be taken out of the way. And then shall* the *Lawless* One *be revealed, whom* the Lord Jesus shall *consume with* the *breath of his mouth, and* shall *destroy with* the *appearance of his coming:* whose *coming is after* the *power of Satan in all* power *and signs* and *wonders of falsehood, and in all deceit of unrighteousness for them that are perishing: because they* received *not the love of the truth, that they might be saved. And for this cause doth* God *send them the* working *of delusion, that they should believe the falsehood: that they may all be judged who believed not the truth, but had pleasure in unrighteousness.'*

Now the first matter to be settled respecting this passage is as to its character, in the mind and intention of the Apostle. Did he intend it for a prophetic declaration of that which should hereafter be, or merely for an expression of his own feelings and apprehensions regarding the course of unbelief? We should not have put the question at all, had not this latter alternative been propounded by some among ourselves, whose names command respect. We will only say, that if we are to adopt it, then, it seems to us, we also adopt a rule of interpretation which will deprive Scripture of any categorical meaning whatever. If ever language was solemn, and declaratory of divine purpose, this is so. We are told to compare, by way of corroborating the view that St. Paul was merely speaking his own feelings and apprehensions, his language in Acts xx. 29, "For I know that after my departure grievous wolves shall enter in among you, not sparing the flock. Yea, of your own selves shall men arise, speaking perverse things, to draw away disciples after them;' and that in 2 Tim. i. 15, 'This thou knowest, that all they which are in Asia be turned away from me.' Surely a more unfortunate reference could not be made. For what two modes of speaking could be more different than that of those places where he is speaking his own convictions and sad experiences, and that adopted here? The reference itself is a refutation. He is clearly, to any unbiassed reader, speaking here in the fulness of apostolic power; as when, in the former Epistle, he said, 'This we declare unto you by the word of the Lord.' That about which they had gone wrong, was an event of world-wide import, even the second advent of the Lord. And his correction of their error was of course made 'in like material,' or it would have been no correction at all. He informs them of matters hidden in the divine counsels, but revealed to him by the Spirit, —matters which might tend to convince them, and through them the Church in all time, that the day of the Lord is not yet manifested, nor shall be until certain appointed developments of evil shall have taken place. We lay it down then for our readers fearlessly, that the passage is prophetic: is the language of the Holy Ghost to the Church, to us, respecting that which is to be gone through before the day of the Lord.

This, then, being laid down, what is it which is declared?

Let the reader carefully observe that there are three things, or rather, perhaps, two, which require to be interpreted :—1. The apostasy; 2. The man of sin, or of lawlessness; and 3. 'That which,' and 'he which,' 'hinders' the manifestation of this man of sin. I said 'rather perhaps two,' because the former two, the *apostasy*, and the *man of sin*, are so closely connected, that they may almost be regarded as one. The *man of sin* is some great concentration of the principle of the apostasy, be he official, or be he individual.

First, then, what is '*the apostasy*'? The question must be answered, not by preconceived views, nor by traditional prejudices, but simply by fair consideration of the passage before us. The apostasy must be judged by the place which it here occupies, and by the characteristics in which it culminates. The place which it occupies is immediately before the coming of the Lord: and it is pointed out as *the* apostasy, because it will be the greatest of all apostasies; that one to which all others will converge, and in which they will be absorbed. Now we may fearlessly say, that such an apostasy, in its full development, the world has not yet seen. There have been many 'fallings away' since the Lord was received into heaven. There were the partial revivals of paganism under Julian and others: there was the great Mahommedan imposture, drawing after it the greater portion of the East. Churches have left their faith and been extinguished: heresies have sprung up and run their course. In the Eastern and Western churches, corruption of doctrine and practice has set in. In the latter especially a monstrous caricature of Christianity has put itself in the place of the faith once delivered to the Church: a local bishop has set himself over churches and kingdoms; has invented new doctrines, or borrowed the cast-off abominations of paganism. A more subtle method of undermining the gospel of Christ has never been devised; but still the Papacy is not '*the apostasy*,' any more than any one of the others mentioned. The Papacy does not, which the apostasy must do, abjure and cast off Christ. The power of Christ's Spirit, however thwarted by its systematic violation and perversion of truth, lives in its system, and works, by means of the sacred Word, on the hearts of its members. To deny this is to shut our eyes to the most manifest and blessed facts.

In a word, *the apostasy* is yet to be manifested. Its form cannot be doubtful; its preparations are going on, and have long been, among the nations of Christendom. It is not any corrupt form of Christianity; it is not Mahommedanism, with its firm hold on the unity and sovereignty of God; but it *is* the spread of secular unbelief, which denies, and casts off, God: which sets up nature above God, physical law above personal will. It is the idolatry of material force and of human genius, as opposed to the revelation of the divine and supernatural. That each of the lesser apo stasies has ministered and is ministering to the preparation of this great one, is manifest: and none more signally than the Papacy, with its speaking of lies in hypocrisy, and its universal debasement of the sense of truth and of moral feeling. Any one need but mingle in continental society in any country, to see how completely Romanism has subserved unbelief, and how its exaggeration of claims on submission has issued in universal contempt for its dogmas.

THE APOSTASY, then, as we understand it, will be the open and general casting off of Christianity in favour of secular unbelief. How long it will be delayed, God knows; but it is assuredly that to which, sooner or later, the present state of things is tending. What dimensions it will assume, again God knows. It will not carry away, it will not silence, the Church. Rather will the cloud blacken as the sun brightens, and the testimony to Christ among the faithful will be clearer and purer in words and deeds, as the denial of Christ waxes wider and bolder.

But *the apostasy* will come to a *head*. The more men cast off God, the only Master of the human spirit, the more they become the prey of *man*.

And not only this. 'In proportion as the general standard of mental cultivation is raised, and man made equal with man, the ordinary power of genius is diminished, but its extraordinary power is increased; its reach deepened, its hold made more firm. As men become familiar with the achievements and the exercise of talent, they learn to despise and disregard its daily examples, and to be more independent of mere men of ability; but they only become more completely in the power of gigantic intellect, and the slaves of pre-eminent and unapproachable talent.'*

This being so, there seems nothing improbable, *à priori*, in the apostasy culminating in the person of some one personal representative. Every one of its partial manifestations which we have already seen has done so from time to time. And with this idea the plain words of the prophecy completely tally. The 'lawless One' here spoken of, is most naturally understood, not as a dynasty, or an official succession, but as an individual man. Thus the early interpreters always understood the expression. 'There was nothing in their peculiar

---

* I quote from the Introduction to my "New Testament for English Readers," vol. ii. p. 92.

circumstances or temperament which prevented them from interpreting all that is here said as a personification, or from allegorising it, as others have done since. This fact gives their interpretation an historical weight, the inference from which it is difficult to escape. The subject of the coming of Antichrist must have been no uncommon one in preaching and writing, during the latter part of the first, and the second century. That no echoes of the apostolic sayings on the matter should have reached thus far, no savour of the first outpouring of interpretation by the Spirit penetrated through the next generation, can hardly be conceived.'

We assume then that this Man of sin, or of lawlessness, is an individual, who shall arise out of the apostasy, and gain to himself the power over its component elements. Let it surprise none that such things as 'sitting in the temple of God and showing himself that he is God,' are predicated of him. From unbelief comes lawlessness; contempt of moral restraint which rests on divine sanction; and from casting off of men's legitimate Ruler and Guide, united to the degradation of man's soul consequent on immorality, comes gross superstition; fetish worship, under the guise of derision of worship; readiness to bow down to any usurper, when the rightful monarch has been dethroned.

But there was a *hindrance* to the manifestation of this Man of sin when the Apostle wrote; and that hindrance is still unremoved; and there was a *hinderer*, in whom that hindrance was embodied. The Fathers, in early times, took these respectively as being the Roman Empire, and he that ruled it. I believe they were right. But they judged for their own times; we must judge for ours. That empire, in the form which they witnessed, has past away. But its 'hindrance' has been continued, in other forms. It has given place to other empires and kingdoms, by whose means the Christian churches have been maintained, and the reign of law and order has been ensured. As often as the partial outbreaks of lawlessness have taken place, these temporal powers have given way before them; and when human society again returned to its usual course, it has been by the knitting up again, in new combinations, of the fabric of state governments. Their power, wherever the seeds of evil are most plentiful, is strictly a *coercive* power;

and there only is its restraining hand able to be relaxed, where the light and liberty of the Gospel are shed abroad. And this temporal power has ever been especially in conflict with the Papacy, restraining its pretensions, modifying its course of action, witnessing more or less against its tyranny and its lies.

If this interpretation be correct, 'he that hindereth' will be that person, whoever he might be, then at the head of the hindering power. At the time when the Apostle wrote, this was the Roman Emperor, supreme over the known world: at other times the hindering power might be split up into various portions, and governed by many persons. It would seem from the prophecy that this system of lawful and law-observing power is gradually to be dissolved before the end. The wild excesses of unbelief will then break forth over the Christian world, as they did partially break forth in the suspension of lawful government during the first revolution in France. How long the predestined Man of lawlessness will be in power, is not declared to us. But one thing is certain; that his antagonism against our Lord and his Church will be cut short by the appearing of the Lord himself, which will be his destruction. Thus we are carried on to the time of the end; apparently to the same great conflict of which we read in other parts of the prophetic Scriptures, which shall be terminated by the personal victory of Christ himself over his banded enemies.

That there are many objectors to this interpretation I am well aware; but I cannot say that their objections have great weight with me, as against the consent of the early interpreters, and the general analogy of the language of prophecy. The favourite interpretation of Antichrist is, that it is the Papacy, or the Pope for the time being. But this signally fails to fulfil any of the requisite conditions of the prophecy. For in the first place the Papacy has been, according to these very interpreters, in power for 1260 years, and the Lord is not yet come; a fact which, though it may, by forcing the meaning of words, be reconciled with the language of our prophecy, yet is manifestly, to the fair-judging observer, at variance with its natural acceptation, according to which the manifestation of the Man of sin is immediately to precede Christ's coming. And secondly, so far is the Papacy from answering to the description of 'setting itself up above all that is called God, or worshipped,' that its characteristic is to multiply objects of worship, and to bow down to canonized men and women, to sacred images and winking pictures; in a word, it can never have gods enough nor lords enough; it is an example, not of atheism, but of pleistotheism; Olympus was nothing to the Paradise of Vatican-made deities. Some curious arguments have been used to show that, notwithstanding the Pope's devotion to multitudes of gods, he yet answers to the description here given; because he makes gods, he must be greater than the gods he makes. But this is the merest fallacy, arising from an equivocal use of the verb 'to make.' The making in this sense is not creation, but simply an act of investiture, or conferring a title or office. It would be about as sound an argument to infer that the archbishop who crowns a king is greater than the king; or that a tailor is greater than he who employs him. The Pope gives the most emphatic denial to this character of him, at the very time when he is supposed most to exemplify it. On the occasions when he enters St. Peter's, borne in state on men's shoulders, with his peacocks' fans, and his silver trumpets, he is always set down at the chapel on the right hand as the nave is entered, and spends some time in 'adoring the blessed Sacrament.'

It will excite no surprise in the mind of any believing Christian to read that this Man of lawlessness shall come 'in the power of Satan,' and with the accompaniment of 'signs and wonders.' Those who regard the operations of nature as the mere results of laws independent of personal spiritual agency, may treat such an announcement with contempt; but those only. We of Christ's Church believe that the present course of things is the conflict, on the broad stage of the world, between our Captain, the Lord Jesus Christ, and the great Foe of God and man—the conflict which in person He waged and won when He trod the earth, but which remains to be fought out by them whose souls He has redeemed, and to whom He gives the power of His finished victory for aid. They in their own persons, His Church in her collective capacity, must follow out that victory which He has won: and then when it is about to be finally and gloriously consummated, will the power of evil culminate and do its worst. Then shall the Foe himself try by his agents all his arts, and illude the world with signs and wonders, wrought by permitted power.

And when this reign of darkness is at its height;—when all worship and faith and service of good and of God shall have been abandoned, and the little flock, despised, and perhaps persecuted, shall have dwindled down to the lowest;—when unbelief shall have given way to scorn;—when the very name of Christian shall be held the badge of idiotcy, and the falsehood of the Gospel shall have become clear by a hundred demonstrations:—then shall there arise in the heavens the brightness of His presence whom we love; then shall the 'new day risen upon the day' wax brighter and brighter, till all but they whose eyes are purified to behold it, shrink back, baffled and dazzled. Then shall the foes of light wither away, and be as though they had not been; and He whose name is Light shall stand revealed upon our earth. 'Amen, even so come, Lord Jesus.'

The varieties of the sacred text in this Epistle, deserving attention, are but few.

In chapter i. ver. 2, for 'our Father,' some of our oldest MSS. read 'the Father'; ver. 10, '*believe*' should be 'believed:' as so often, the past is looked back upon as if from that future day.

In ch. ii. 2, 'the day of *Christ*,' should be 'the day of the Lord.' In ver. 3, our two oldest MSS., for '*sin*,' have 'lawlessness.' In ver. 4, the words 'as God' are omitted by all our most ancient MSS. In ver. 8, for '*the Lord*,' most of our oldest MSS., versions, and Fathers, read 'the Lord Jesus.' In ver. 11, for '*God shall send them*,' read 'doth God send them.'

In ch. iii. 6, '*he* received' should be 'they received.'

We now come to consider the places where our Authorised Version has inadequately represented the sacred text.

In ch. i. 7, '*his mighty angels*,' should be 'the angels of his might.' The difference is not important here: but in some places, *e.g.*, Phil. iii. 21, this practice of rendering by an adjective, eclipses and obscures the whole meaning. In ver. 11, for '*the good pleasure of his goodness*,' should stand 'good pleasure of goodness.'

In ch. ii. 1, '*by* the coming,' should be 'touching,' or 'concerning, the coming.' As it now stands, it looks like a formula of adjuring them with which the phrase has nothing to do. In ver. 2, 'shaken *in mind*' should be 'shaken from your mind.' In the same verse, '*is at hand*' should be 'is come.' This has been vehemently denied by several who have differed from the above interpretation of the passage. But it appears to me that the words can mean nothing else. The verb occurs six times besides in the New Testament, and always with the meaning, 'to be *present*,' not, 'to be *at hand*.' It is the same word as that in the expression 'things present or things to come' in Rom. viii. 38 and 1 Cor. iii. 22 and is thus distinguished from any reference to the future. And so Chrysostom, himself a Greek, and knowing the force of his own language: 'The devil, when he could not persuade them that the announcements of things future were false, took another way, and having suborned certain pestilent fellows, endeavoured to deceive by persuading them that those great and glorious events had an end. At one time they said that the resurrection was already past (2 Tim. ii. 17, 18): but in this case they said that the judgment was come, and the presence of Christ . . . thus removing fear of retribution for the evil, and hope of reward for the good. In ver. 3, for '*a falling away*,' render 'the apostasy.' It is not one among many apostasies, but *the* great and well-known one, which is indicated. The article, being expressed in the Greek in a place where it could not but be emphatic, ought never to have been omitted by our translators. In ver. 8, '*spirit*' is better 'breath': and '*brightness*' ought to be 'appearance.' In ver. 9, 'lying wonders' should have been 'wonders of falsehood' (see above on ch. i. 7). In ver. 11, '*a lie*' ought to have been 'the falsehood': viz., that before spoken of. In ver. 12, '*damned*' ought to be 'judged.' The word in the original is simply that, and nothing more. Of course, from the context, both in the Greek and in the English, an *unfavourable* issue of the judgment must be assumed: but the word never ought to have been strengthened in the translation, either here or in the other places where it has been similarly treated (one very sad instance occurs in 1 Cor. xi. 29). In ver. 13, '*through* sanctification' ought to be 'in sanctification.' Sanctification is not the instrument, but the necessary conditioning state, of our salvation. A similar inaccuracy occurs in ver. 16, where '*through* grace' ought to be 'in grace.'

In ch. iii. 2, 'perverse' more nearly answers to the force of the Greek adjective than *'unreasonable'*: and *'faith'* should be 'the faith.' In ver. 5, *'the patient waiting for* Christ' ought to be 'the patience of Christ,' the patience which was in Christ. The words will not bear the other rendering. In ver. 7 (also in ver. 9), *'follow'* ought to be 'imitate.' In ver. 8, *'for nought'* is perhaps not quite clear: it may give the impression that 'without result' is meant: 'without recompense,' or 'without payment,' would express the meaning more perspicuously. In ver. 11, in the words 'working not at all, but are busy-bodies,' there is in the original a play upon words, which it is a pity to lose altogether: 'working at no business, but being busybodies,' comes as near as perhaps can be accomplished in English. In ver. 12, '*by* our Lord Jesus Christ' should be '*in* our Lord Jesus Christ.' In ver. 16, '*by all means*' should be 'in every way.'

I may add, that the probable date of the writing of the two Epistles to the Thessalonians is between the years 52 and 54 A.D. In the latter of these two years, Nero succeeded Claudius as Emperor of Rome.

IV.

THE FIRST EPISTLE TO THE CORINTHIANS.

WE left St. Paul at Corinth, where his sojourn lasted eighteen months. In his contentions with the Jews there he had been comforted by a vision, in which the Lord had assured him that He had much people in that city. And so he remained, teaching the word of God, till the stir arose in which the cautious and amiable Gallio, refusing to notice the complaints of the Jews, had ensured for the new faith the protection of the law. This favourable incident enabled the Apostle to prolong his stay yet further. His ultimate departure appears to have been occasioned by a vow, compelling him to visit Jerusalem. Thither he rapidly proceeded, making a short visit at Ephesus by the way, and (for we hurry on to the scene with which we are now concerned) returning through Antioch, and the central countries of Asia Minor, again to Ephesus. There he made the longest stay of any recorded during his missionary journeys; no less than three whole years, as he himself describes it. During this time a visit to Corinth took place, which has not been recorded in the Acts. In 2 Cor. xii. 14, xiii. 1, he tells them that he was coming to them *the third time*, which would of course imply that he had visited them twice before. But only one previous visit has been related, viz., that first one, during which he wrote the Epistles to the Thessalonians. Before his next recorded visit, viz., that mentioned in Acts xx. 1, 2, both the Epistles to the Corinthians had been written. He wrote the *first* from Ephesus, at a time when he intended to stay there till Pentecost, 1 Cor. xvi. 8: he wrote the second from Macedonia, at a time when he had recently left Asia, 2 Cor. ix. 1—4; i. 8; ii. 12—after being there in danger of his life. All this agrees with the history of his sojourn in Ephesus related in Acts xix., and with his journey through Macedonia, related Acts xx. 1, 2. We infer then that he must have gone over from Ephesus to Corinth at some time early in those three years of his Ephesian visit. Nor need we be in the least degree surprised that this journey is not recorded in the Acts. For this is the case with numerous travels and adventures of the Apostle. Long and important journeys are dismissed in a few words (see ch. xv. 41, xvi. 6, xviii. 23, xix. 1, xx. 2, 3), or even altogether omitted, as that to Arabia, mentioned Gal. i. 17, and that in Syria and Cilicia, Gal. i. 21. Of the long catalogue of perils given by him in 2 Cor. xi. 24—26, very few can be identified in the history. Ephesus and Corinth were the usual points of transit to and from Asia and Europe,* and a journey across and back might present very little for the sacred historian to dwell upon.

The *nature* of this visit is important for those who would understand these Epistles aright. It is alluded to in 2 Cor. ii. 1, as having been made '*in heaviness*,'—for some reason which gave him sorrow of heart; evidently, the unworthy behaviour of some among the Corinthians: for he tells them (2 Cor. xiii. 2, rightly rendered) that during it, he warned them that if he came again 'he

---

* Dean Howson compares them to Liverpool and New York; and the time of transit eleven days, also corresponded.

would not spare" (the sinners); and there is a hint (2 Cor. xii. 21) that during it, God had 'humbled him among them.'

But we may gather more notices of the state of the Corinthian church at this second visit. In 2 Cor. xii. 21, these words occur: '*Lest, when I come again, my God will humble me among you, and that I shall bewail many which have sinned already, and have not repented of the uncleanness and fornication and lasciviousness which they have committed.*' These were the besetting sins of the place; and the same great peril had set in here which so generally accompanied the infancy of the primitive churches, that of converts, while their convictions and professions were with the church, neglecting to reform their impure heathenish practices. I have said elsewhere—'It was a visit unpleasant in the process and in recollection: perhaps very short, and as sad as short: in which he seems merely to have thrown out solemn warnings of the consequences of a future visit of apostolic severity if the abuses were persisted in,—and possibly to have received insult from some among them on account of such warning.'*

---

* "New Testament for English Readers," Introduction to 1 Cor.

This unrecorded visit was followed up, on the Apostle's return to Ephesus, by an Epistle, now lost to us. We might have inferred from hints given in the first Epistle, that such had been the case.* But we are put out of doubt by the assertion of ch. v. 9: *I wrote to you in an* (properly, *in my*) *Epistle, not to keep company with fornicators.*' No such command occurs in the earlier part of 1 Cor., to which alone, if not to another Epistle, reference could be made.

An objection has been raised to the idea of such a lost Epistle having existed, of which I can only say, that it is childish and ridiculous, and can hardly be mentioned with too severe reprobation. It proceeds on the assumption that no apostolic writing can ever have been lost. I have before observed (p. 9) that the same absurd assumption would require that all apostolic *sayings* should have been preserved to us; for surely these were as precious, and as much inspired by God, as the others. But this whole class of *à priori* objections and assumptions is beneath, as it is beyond,

---

* See ch. xvi. 1, whence it would appear that injunctions to make a collection for the saints had at some time been given by the Apostle. As further instructions were needed now to carry these out, they can hardly have been given *vivâ voce*.

refutation. There are no more mischievous obstructors of truth among us, than the maintainers of a system in which God's duties, and not ours, are the starting point. Judging from the actual phenomena of our existing Epistles, it is highly probable that not one only, but many others, have been lost. Are we to suppose, for instance, that the Epistle to Philemon was the only 'personal' letter St. Paul ever wrote? And what has become of the Epistle which the Colossians were to get from Laodicea and read in their assembly (Col. iv. 16)? And when we find St. Paul proposing to give commendatory letters to the messengers of the churches (the right rendering of 1 Cor. xvi. 3), are we not to suppose that this was his usual practice?

Believing then that an Epistle, now lost to us, followed on this unhappy second visit to Corinth, we can easily trace its temper and contents. He had in it given them a command '*not to keep company with fornicators*' (1 Cor. v. 9). It contained an account of his plan of visiting them on his way to Macedonia, and again on his return from Macedonia (2 Cor. i. 15, 16): a plan which he afterwards changed in consequence of the bad news received from Corinth (1 Cor. xvi. 5—7); for which alteration of plan he was charged with lightness of purpose (2 Cor. i. 17). It evidently included also an order to make a collection for the poor saints at Jerusalem (see above). 'It was a short letter, containing perhaps little or nothing more than the above announcement and injunctions, given, probably, in the pithy and sententious manner so common with the Apostle.'*

It would appear (see above) that the unrecorded visit occurred somewhat early in the three years spent at Ephesus. For after it there had been time, before the writing of this Epistle, for new troubles and difficulties to arise in the Corinthian church, and for a letter to be written, and perhaps also a deputation sent, to the Apostle (see 1 Cor. vii. 1, i. 11, xvi. 17), to obtain his decision on some doubtful points, or to lay the state of the church before him.

Supposing St. Paul to have arrived at Ephesus late in the year 54, we might venture to place the unrecorded journey to Corinth in the spring of 55, and the writing of this Epistle in the spring of 57. Of one thing we are certain: that

* "New Testament for English Readers," Introduction to 1 Cor.

it was written early in the same year in which he left Ephesus for Macedonia (1 Cor. xvi. 8).

We now come to the Epistle itself. Its immediate occasion seems to have been, the arrival at Ephesus of the family, or some of the family, of a Christian matron at Corinth, named Chloe. These had brought, perhaps the letter of inquiries, but certainly unfavourable intelligence (ch. i. 11) from the Corinthian church. The Apostle names only the report of divisions and parties: but we can hardly be wrong in believing that the news of the very serious matter treated in ch. v. were brought by the same persons. These tidings, together with the questions on which apostolic counsels were requested, induced St. Paul to write this, one of the longest and most important of his pastoral letters, and the pattern, above all others, of earnest and weighty admonition and declaration springing out of circumstances. For of such a character, above all others, is this our Epistle,—not a treatise on any point or any system of Christian doctrine, as some others by this same Apostle, but a series of fragments, or episodes, each of them *occasional*, arising out of something referred to him, or heard of by him, but not one of them devoid of interest for those who come after in all the long ages of the Church.

I offer no apology for transcribing here the section 'On the matter and style' of this Epistle in my Introduction to vol. iii. of my "New Testament for English Readers":—

'As might have been expected from the occasion of writing, the matter of this Epistle is very various. It is admirably characterised by Mr. Conybeare, in Conybeare and Howson's "Life and Epistles of St. Paul," vol. ii. p. 28 (2nd edition):—

'"This letter is, in its contents, the most diversified of all St. Paul's Epistles: and in proportion to the variety of its topics, is the depth of its interest for ourselves. For by it we are introduced as it were behind the scenes of the apostolic Church, and its minutest features are revealed to us under the light of daily life. We see the picture of a Christian congregation as it met for worship in some upper chamber, such as the house of Aquila or of Gaius could furnish. We see that these seasons of pure devotion were not unalloyed by human vanity and excitement: yet, on the other hand, we behold the heathen auditor pierced to the heart by the inspired eloquence of the Christian prophets, the secrets of his conscience laid bare to him, and himself constrained to fall down on his face and worship God : we hear the fervent thanksgiving echoed by the unanimous Amen : we see the administration of the Holy Communion terminating the feast of love. Again, we become familiar with the perplexities of domestic life, the corrupting proximity of heathen immorality, the lingering superstition, the rash speculation, the lawless perversion of Christian liberty : we witness the strife of theological factions, the party names, the sectarian animosities. We perceive the difficulty of the task imposed upon the Apostle, who must guard from so many perils, and guide through so many difficulties, his children in the faith, whom else he had begotten in vain : and we learn to appreciate more fully the magnitude of that laborious responsibility under which he describes himself as almost ready to sink, 'the care of all the churches.'

'" But while we rejoice that so many details of the deepest historical interest have been preserved to us by this Epistle, let us not forget to thank God, who so inspired his Apostle that in his answers to questions of transitory interest he has laid down principles of eternal obligation. Let us trace with gratitude the providence of Him, who 'out of darkness calls up light;' by whose mercy it was provided that the unchastity of the Corinthians should occasion the sacred laws of moral purity to be established for ever through the Christian world:—that their denial of the resurrection should cause those words to be recorded whereon reposes, as upon a rock that cannot be shaken, our sure and certain hope of immortality."

'In style, this Epistle ranks perhaps the foremost of all as to sublimity and earnest and impassioned eloquence. Of the former, the description of the simplicity of the Gospel in ch. ii.,—the concluding apostrophe of ch. iii. (ver. 16—end), the same in ch. vi. (ver. 9—end),—the reminiscence of the shortness of the time, ch. vii. 29—31,—the whole argument in ch. xv., are examples unsurpassed in Scripture itself: and of the latter, ch. iv. 8—15, and the whole of ch. ix.: while the panegyric of Love, in ch. xiii., stands a pure and perfect gem, perhaps the noblest assemblage of beautiful thoughts in beautiful language extant in this our world. —About the whole Epistle there is a character of lofty and sustained solemnity,—an absence of tortuousness of construction, and an apologetic plainness, which contrast remarkably with the personal portions of the second Epistle.

'No Epistle raises in us a higher estimate of the varied and wonderful gifts with which God was pleased to endow the man whom He selected for the Apostle of the Gentile world: or shows us how large a portion of the Spirit, who worketh in each man severally as He will, was given to him for our edification. The depths of the spiritual, the moral, the intellectual, the physical world are open to him. He summons to his aid the analogies of nature. He enters minutely into the varieties of human infirmity and prejudice. He draws warning from the history of the chosen people: example from the Isthmian foot-race. He refers an apparently trifling question of costume to the first great proprieties and relations of Creation and Redemption. He praises, reproves, exhorts, and teaches. Where he strikes he heals. His large heart holding all, where he has grieved any, he grieves likewise; where it is in his power to give joy, he first overflows with joy himself. We may form some idea from this Epistle better perhaps than from any one other,—because this embraces the widest range of topics,—what marvellous power such a man must have had to persuade, to rebuke, to attract and fasten the affections of men.'

I now proceed to give an analysis of the contents of the Epistle, commenting shortly on the various points of interest as we proceed. After the opening salutation and expression of thankfulness for God's grace given to the Corinthians, the Apostle at once proceeds to treat of the divisions among them, of which he had learned from 'Chloe's people.' These divisions have been commonly understood to have taken the form of regular parties or sects; and the German writers have spent a great deal of ingenuity in minutely describing the Cephas-party, the Paul-party, the Apollos-party, the Christ-party. But this is hardly justified by the text. All we can assume is that certain persons had arisen as teachers antagonistic to St. Paul, and claiming superiority to him on various accounts: some as representing the teaching of St. Peter, an elder and greater Apostle: some as following the Alexandrine learning of Apollos: some again, as having had the advantage of nearer personal intercourse with Christ himself: while the followers of Paul were degenerating into the same type of a mere personal adhesion to *him*, instead of following him as he followed Christ. This confused embryo state of parties appears to have been all that can be safely assumed. And this appears the case by the subsequent epistle of Clement, bishop of Rome, to the Corinthians, in which we find no vestige of any of these parties, but only the far commoner faults of insubordination and ambition.

This subject, and the consequent explanation and vindication of the Apostle's teaching, occupies him as far as the end of the fourth chapter, which he ends with a threat of soon coming among them, and vindicating his apostolic power.

Then, in ch. v. he deals with the gross case of moral delinquency which had been reported to him, and gives direction for the separation of the offender from the communion of the church. In doing this he takes occasion to correct, or rather to qualify, what he had written in his Epistle sent before this; drawing a distinction between the fornicators of this world, with whom they must needs have ordinary commerce, and Christian brethren guilty of such sin, with whom they were to keep no company whatever.

Chap. vi. is of a mixed character. It would

appear that this case of the incestuous person had in some way given occasion for proceeding in the heathen courts of law respecting a matter in which the Christian Church ought to have pronounced judgment. We gather this from the circumstance of the Apostle's returning again to the subject of fornication, after he had spoken against calling in the heathen to judge between Christians.

Chap. vii. is devoted to answering an enquiry which they had addressed to him, respecting the expediency of marriage. It is one of those passages commonly supposed only to have reference to the time for which it was written, but in reality full of weighty counsel for all ages of the Church. Some of the matters in it, which appear obscure in our English version, will be found cleared up in the notices at the end of this article.

In ch. viii.—x. he deals with another question which they had referred to him, the lawfulness of partaking of meats which had been specially dedicated to idols, by forming part of animals sacrificed to them. Viewed in the abstract, there could be no doubt that such dedication was null and void, an idol being a mere fiction of a non-existent being. But such questions are not to be viewed in the abstract. Harm may be done, not only by doing that which is wrong in itself, but by doing that which seems wrong to another man, and which if done by him after our example, would be against his conscience, and therefore, to him, an act of sin. He shows in ch. ix. how he himself abstained, on account of the conscience of others, from things otherwise lawful for him: how he, far from inquiring how much indulgence he might take for the flesh, kept under his body, and brought it into subjection, as one running for a prize. Then in ch. x. he goes into another aspect of the same question, showing them the peril of commerce with idolatry, by the history of Israel of old, and by the nature of the communion which we have with Christ and one another in the bread and the cup of the great Christian sacrament: concluding with definite directions how to act in doubtful cases, and a general exhortation to avoid giving offence to any.

Chap. xi. deals with two matters. First, the question of the costume of women in the Christian assemblies; and secondly, the abuses which had crept into the administration of the Lord's Supper among them. In treating this latter, the Apostle takes occasion to deliver, as from the Lord himself, a detailed account of the institution of that holy ordinance.

With ch. xii. begins the Apostle's instruction respecting 'spiritual gifts.' The 'occasional' interest of this part of the Epistle was confined to the apostolic period; but, as usual, in the course of his explanation he continually expounds principles and gives directions, applicable alike to all ages of the Church.

But the chief interest of this portion of the Epistle is the occurrence in it of the glorious panegyric on Christian Love, in ch. xiii. Good and desirable as all spiritual gifts are, there is a way of doing God's work and serving his glory super-eminent above them all, namely, Love—the only law for all time and all eternity. I may be allowed to add to what has been already said on this chapter, the remarks of Dean Stanley in his Commentary on these Epistles: 'On each side of this chapter the tumult of argument and remonstrance still rages: but within it, all is calm: the sentences move in almost rhythmical melody; the imagery unfolds itself in almost dramatic propriety; the language arranges itself with almost rhetorical accuracy. We can imagine how the Apostle's amanuensis must have paused to look up in his master's face at the sudden change in the style of his dictation, and seen his countenance lighted up as it had been the face of an angel, as this vision of divine perfection passed before him.'

As ch. xii. contained the general theory of the supernatural gifts then extant in the Church, ch. xiv. comprises practical directions how to deal with the same, that they might be decorously and profitably exercised.

Chap. xv. is reserved for the treatment of a great foundation doctrine of Christianity, the Resurrection of the Body. Seeing that this doctrine was repudiated by some at Corinth, it became necessary that it should be thoroughly expounded, as to its grounds, its analogies, its necessity. And thus we obtain one of the grandest and most precious portions of the apostolic writings. For record of the appearances of the Lord after His resurrection,—for cogent argument binding His resurrection to ours,—for assertion and implication of the great doctrine of His inclusive Humanity,—for revelation of holy mysteries imparted by special inspiration,—for triumphant application of the phenomena and analogies of nature,—no extant writing can compare with this chapter in its value to the Church,—its power of convincing the mind and awakening Christian hope,—its far-seeing confutation of the cavils and scoffs of all after-ages against the doctrine of the Resurrection.

The sixteenth chapter is supplementary, consisting entirely of particular directions, personal notices, and short notes of encouragement and warning.

I hasten to the task, considerable in so long an Epistle, of pointing out the changes made necessary in the English text by more correct readings and renderings. First, for those places in which our version is made from a text not agreeing with our most ancient authorities.

In ch. i. 22, '*a sign*' should be 'signs.' In ver. 23, '*Greeks*' should be 'Gentiles.' In ver. 28, '*yea and things*' should be 'the things.' In ver. 29, '*in his presence*' should be 'before God.'

In ch. ii. 4, it is uncertain whether the word 'man's' should be inserted or omitted. The most ancient MSS. are divided on the point. In ver. 13, for '*which the Holy Ghost teacheth*' read 'in words taught by the Spirit.'

In ch. iii. 3, '*and divisions*' should be omitted.*
In ver. 4, for '*carnal*' read 'men,' *i.e.*, walking merely as men, not as Christians : see on chap. xv. 32. In ver. 13, after 'the fire,' add 'itself.'

Chap. iv. 2, after 'stewards' insert 'here ;' *i.e.*, here on earth, in worldly matters.

Chap. v. 1, for '*is not so much as named* among the Gentiles' read 'is not even among the Gentiles.' Ver. 3, for '*as absent*' read 'being absent.' Ver. 4 (1st time), omit '*Christ.*' Ver. 5 (end), omit '*Jesus.*' Ver. 7, omit '*therefore.*' Ver. 10, omit '*yet :*' and for '*or*' (2nd time) read 'and.' Ver. 13, omit '*Therefore.*'

Chap. vi. 20 (end), omit the words '*and in your spirit, which are God's.*'

Chap. vii. 3, for '*due benevolence*' read 'her due.' Ver. 5, omit '*fasting and :*' and for '*come* together' read 'be together.' Ver. 13, for '*him*' read 'her husband.' Ver. 14, for '*by the husband*' read 'in the brother ;' *i.e.*, is sanctified, in that the believing brother is her husband. Ver. 38, for '*but*' read 'and.' Ver. 39, omit '*by the law.*'

Chap. ix. 1 should stand, 'Am I not free ? Am

---

* These words have been left, by oversight, in the text of my "New Testament for English Readers."

I not an apostle?' Ver. 10, for '*he that thresheth in hope should be partaker of his hope,*' read 'he that thresheth [should thresh], in hope of partaking.' Ver. 16, for '*Yea, woe,*' read 'for woe.' Ver. 18, omit '*of Christ.*' Ver. 20, after the words 'to them that are under the law as under the law,' insert 'not being myself under the law.' Ver. 23, for '*this* I do' read 'all things I do.'

Chap. x. 1, for '*Moreover*' read 'For.' Ver. 9, for '*Christ*' read 'the Lord,' and omit '*also;*' as likewise in ver. 10. Ver. 11, instead of '*for ensamples*' read 'by way of figure,' or 'example.' Ver. 20, for '*the Gentiles*' read 'they.' Ver. 23, omit '*for me*' both times. Ver. 28, omit '*unto idols:*' also omit, *in this verse*, '*for the earth is the Lord's, and the fulness thereof.*' Ver. 30, omit '*for.*'

Chap. xi. 18, for '*in the church*' read 'in assembly.' Ver. 24, omit '*Take, eat.*' Also omit '*broken;*' reading 'This is my body which is for you.' Ver. 26, for '*this* cup' read 'the cup.' Ver. 29, omit '*unworthily.*' Also omit '*Lord's,*' reading 'the body.' Ver. 34, omit '*And*' at the beginning.

Chap. xii. 2, read 'that when ye were Gentiles,

ye were carried away,' &c. Ver. 3, read 'saith Jesus is accursed.' Ver. 9 (end), for '*the same* Spirit' read 'the one Spirit.' Ver. 12, for '*that one* body' read 'the body.' Ver. 13, for '*into* one Spirit' read 'of one Spirit.' Ver. 31, for 'the *best* gifts' read 'the greatest gifts.'

Chap. xiii. 3, three of our oldest MSS. instead of 'that I may be burned' read 'that I may boast.' The difference in Greek is only that of one letter (*Kauthesomai* and *Kauchesomai*). Ver. 10, omit '*then*.' Ver. 11, omit '*but*.'

Chap. xiv. 18, omit '*my*' before 'God.' Ver. 25, for '*and these are* the secrets of his heart' read 'the secrets of his heart are.' Ver. 35, for '*women*' read 'a woman.'

Chap. xv. 20, omit '*and become*.' Ver. 24, for '*shall have delivered*' read 'delivereth.' Ver. 29 (end), for '*the dead*' read 'them.' In ver. 44 the latter clause should stand, 'If there is a natural body, there is also a spiritual.' In ver. 47, omit '*the Lord*.' In ver. 49 most of our ancient MSS. read, for 'we shall also bear,' 'let us also bear:' but the Vatican MS. and ancient Syriac version read as our text. In ver. 51 many ancient authorities read, 'We shall all sleep, but we shall not all be changed.' But here again the Vatican MS. and ancient Syriac version have it as our text. In ver. 55, for '*grave*' read again 'death.'

In ch. xvi. 7, for 'but' read 'for.' In ver. 22 omit '*Jesus Christ*.'

The principal places in which our translators have wrongly or inadequately rendered the text, are the following :—

Chap. i. 26 should stand, 'How that not many of you are wise after the flesh, not many mighty, not many noble.'

Chap. ii. 9, 10, ought to stand, 'But as it is written, Things which eye hath not seen, ear hath not heard, and which have not entered into the heart of man, things which God hath prepared for them that love him, hath God revealed unto us through his Spirit.' Ver. 11, '*no man*' should be 'none.' In ver. 13, '*comparing spiritual with spiritual*,' should be 'interpreting spiritual things to the spiritual.' In ver. 15 (twice), for '*judgeth*' substitute 'discerneth :' and for '*of no man*,' 'by none.'

Chap. iii. 1, for '*carnal*' should stand 'men of flesh.' The word is not that commonly used to signify 'carnal,' but a grosser word, meaning 'made of mere flesh.' In ver. 9, for 'labourers together with God,' should stand 'God's fellow labourers,' *i.e.*, fellow labourers belonging to God. Ver. 14 '*reward*' should be 'wages:' otherwise, the comparison to workmen is confused. Ver. 15, '*by* fire' should be 'through fire.' Ver. 17, 'which temple ye are' ought to be 'the which [viz., holy] ye are.' Ver. 19, '*He taketh*' should be 'He that taketh.'

Chap. iv. 3, '*man's judgment*' should be 'the day of man's judgment.' Ver. 4, '*by* myself' should be 'against myself.' When our version was made, 'by myself' had this meaning, as may be seen in the comments and sermons of the time. 'I know no harm by him' is even now a common expression in some parts of England.* Ver. 5, 'have *praise* of God' should be 'have his praise [that praise which belongs to him] from God. As it stands in the English version, the assertion is not true: *every man* shall not have praise from God. Ver. 6, 'not to *think of men* above that which is written' should be 'not to go beyond what is written.' Ver. 16, '*followers*' should be 'imitators.'

* See my " Queen's English," paragraph 319.

Chap. v. 9, '*in an epistle*' should be 'in my epistle.'

Chap. vi. 9, '*the unrighteous*' should be 'doers of wrong.' It is the same term as above, and takes up the sense. Ver. 11, '*ye are washed*' should be 'ye washed them off,' viz., in your baptism. The *passive* translation is a blunder in grammar. Ver. 15, '*take*' should be 'take away.' Ver. 20, for '*are* brought' substitute 'were brought.'

Chap. vii. 11, '*if she depart*' should be 'if she be actually separated,' *i.e.*, if separation have taken place previously to the arrival of this Epistle. The last clause of the verse ought to stand, 'and that the husband leave not his wife.' Ver. 21 ought to stand, 'Wast thou called being a slave? Care not for it: nay, even if thou canst be made free, use it [slavery] rather': *i.e.*, 'abide in the calling wherein thou wast called.' As the English version now stands, it bears a sense directly contrary to that which the Apostle is enjoining; viz., the sense that the slave should *get liberated if he could*, which would be to *desert* the calling wherein he was called. Throughout this passage '*servant*' should be 'slave': otherwise the strong recommendation of the Apostle is weakened. Ver. 31, '*abusing it* should be 'using it to the full,' using it as if it were all, and they were bound to get all they can out of it. In verses 36 and 37, 'his *virgin*' should be 'his virgin daughter.' The case supposed is that of a father, doubtful whether he shall or shall not give his daughter in marriage. 'Them' of course means the girl and her lover. As the verses stand in the English version, they are simply unintelligible.

Chap. viii. 4, '*that an idol is nothing in the world*' should be 'that there is no idol in the world.' Ver. 8, '*commendeth us not*' ought to be 'shall not be reckoned to us:' *i.e.*, will not affect our future standing.

Chap. ix. 3, '*a sister, a wife*,' is better expressed 'a [believing] sister as a wife.' As the words stand, they are ambiguous. In ver. 9, 'Doth God take care for oxen?' should be, 'Is it for the oxen that God careth' (viz., when He gives this command)? As the words stand, they convey an inference the opposite of truth. The faithful rendering of the definite article makes all the difference. In ver. 17, '*a dispensation of the gospel* is committed unto me' should be 'I have a stewardship entrusted to me.' Ver. 23 (end), 'with *you*' should probably be 'with them.' Nothing is expressed in the original except 'that I may become a fellow-partaker thereof.' In ver. 25, '*Striveth for the mastery*' should be 'contendeth in the games.' In ver. 27 the word rendered '*keep under*' signifies to bruise, to beat black and blue: 'chastise' would be, perhaps, the nearest English.

Chap. x. 5, '*many* of them' should be 'the more part,' or 'the greater part, of them.' Ver. 13, 'also make' would be better 'make also.' One sometimes hears 'also' joined to the previous word 'temptation,' and thus made unmeaning. In verses 16 and 17 '*communion*,' should be 'participation.' 'Communion' has now a technical sense, as the name of an ordinance, and thus causes the idea here intended to be lost by the hearer.

Chap. xi. 10, 'power' would be more intelligently expressed 'the token of power,' *i.e.*, the covering, implying that she is under subjection; and thus preserving comeliness in the sight of the holy angels, who are present in the Christian assemblies. Ver. 20, 'this is not to eat the Lord's supper,' may be better rendered 'there is no eating [*i.e.*, it is not possible to eat] the Lord's [emphasis on this] supper.' Ver. 26, 'ye do *shew*

should be 'ye declare,' or 'announce.' In ver. 27, '*and* drink' is a misrendering, and it is to be feared a wilful one, on the part of our translators. The sacred text stands, 'or drink.' But this seemed to countenance the Romanist error that the partaking in one kind only was a reception of the whole, and therefore apparently 'or' was altered to '*and*.'*
In ver. 29, '*damnation*' should be 'judgment.' It is a disgrace to the Church in England that this most unjustifiable word still remains in the text. It is not only a false rendering of the original, but is at variance with the next verse, which shows that it is not 'damnation' which is intended, but temporal judgments. Of all the English versions, the Rheims (Roman Catholic) is the only one which has been faithful to the sacred text. Our translators condemn themselves, by keeping 'judged' in verses 31, 32; but they have recurred to '*condemnation*' again when they ought to have written 'judgment,' in ver. 34. The boasted perfection of the authorised English version never

---

* It is true that one of our most ancient MSS., the Alexandrine, reads 'and.' But that MS. was not known to our translators: it was presented to Charles I. by Cyril Lucar, patriarch of Constantinople. The alteration from 'or' to 'and' was made first in the Geneva version of 1557. The older English versions all had 'or.'

gives way so completely as in this passage. In ver. 31, 'if we *would judge* ourselves' should be 'if we duly discerned ourselves.' The verb is the same as in 'discern not,' in ver. 29, and should have been carefully kept identical.

In ch. xiv. 2, '*these*' should be 'the.' In ver. 6, '*all in all*' is hardly clear. It would better be 'all in all men.' In ver. 8, the four words rendered '*by*' are different: the first is 'through,' the second 'according to,' the third and fourth 'in.' In ver. 13, '*are* we all baptized' should be 'we were all baptized;' and '*have been* all made' should be 'were all made.' In ch. xiii., '*charity*' might be perhaps rendered 'love.' And yet this is not wholly certain. It may be, that with sufficient and constant explanation, the old term, charity, might better preserve the great idea, and escape the misunderstanding to which the term 'love' might, on one side, be liable. In ver. 11, '*when I became a man, I put away childish things*' should have been, 'now that I am become a man, I have done away the things of the child.' In ver. 12, '*through* a glass' would be more intelligibly expressed in English 'in a glass.' The idea is that of seeing in a mirror; but inasmuch as objects appear on the other side of the mirror, the word 'through' is used. At the end of the verse, 'I *am known*' should be 'I was fully known,' viz., by God.

Chap. xiv. 16, '*occupieth the room of the unlearned*' should be 'is in the situation of a private person:' *i.e.*, is ignorant of these spiritual gifts. And 'amen' should be 'the amen:' *i.e.*, which the whole congregation ordinarily says. The authorised version is barely intelligible. It looks as if the translators had had the *parish clerk* in their minds.* In ver. 24, '*convinced of all*' is liable to be misunderstood; 'convicted by all' is the meaning.

Chap. xv. 8, 'one born out of due time' hardly conveys the idea, which is, that he was the abortive weakling of the apostolic family: 'the one born out of due time' approaches nearer. In ver. 12, '*rose*' should be 'is risen.' In ver. 18, '*are fallen asleep in Christ are perished*' should be 'fell asleep in Christ perished.' In ver. 19, '*have* hope' should be 'have had hope;' and '*miserable*' should be 'to be pitied.' In ver. 27 read, 'But when He shall declare that all things are put in

* Something like this must certainly have been the case with the Rheims version, 'he that supplieth the place of the vulgar.'

subjection, it is manifest that they have been subjected with the exception of Him,' &c. In ver. 29 the punctuation is at fault. It should stand thus: 'Else what shall they do which are baptized for the dead? If the dead rise not at all, why are they then baptized for the dead?' In ver. 31, '*by your rejoicing which I have*' ought to be 'by the glorying which I have of you.' Ver. 32, 'I have fought' should be 'I fought.' The stress in this sentence is on the words 'after the manner of men.' If it were only according to the common ideas of men,—*i.e.*, with no faith in the resurrection. Here, again, the punctuation is wrong. It should stand, 'What doth it profit me? If the dead rise not, let us eat and drink,' &c. In ver. 36, the original requires the emphasis to be laid on 'thou' before 'sowest.' This would be effectually provided for if we rendered, 'that which thou thyself sowest.'

Chap. xvi. 1, '*have given*' should be 'gave.' Ver. 2, 'as God hath prospered him' is better 'whatsoever he be prospered in,' as importing the material in which he is to lay by. '*Gatherings*' would better be expressed 'collections,' a word universally understood. The Apostle sets his face peremptorily against the great sham of charity sermons, and will have no part in stimulating Christians up to their ordinary duty of alms-giving. In ver. 22 there should probably be a full stop at 'Anathema.' Maranatha, 'The Lord cometh,' appears to have been a sort of Christian watchword, having no connection with the word before. Anathema, a curse, is Greek: Maranatha is Hebrew (Aramaic). It would be best to keep the former word in its Greek form, as being more generally understood by us, and to render the latter by, 'The Lord cometh.'

V.

THE SECOND EPISTLE TO THE CORINTHIANS.

ST. PAUL had left Ephesus and crossed into Europe. His departure appears to have been hastened by the tumult of which we read in Acts xix., for immediately after it (xx. 1) we find him passing over into Macedonia. He had heard of the effect produced on the Corinthians by his first Epistle (ch. ii. 3—iii. 8): and was now on his way to them (ch. vii. 14—xiii. 1). He wrote from Macedonia (ch. viii. 1, ix. 2). He had been there some little time, sufficient to have ascertained the mind of the Macedonian churches, and to have gathered from them their contributions for the poor brethren at Jerusalem.

The news of the effect of his former Epistle had been anxiously looked for by him, and he had sent

Titus probably for the purpose of ascertaining it. At Troas, on his way from Ephesus, he had expected to meet Titus (ch. 11. 13), and not finding him there, he crossed into Macedonia, where the meeting took place, and the expected tidings were announced to him. The general reception given to his letter had been favourable, but all had not submitted themselves quietly to it.* The well disposed had been humbled by his reproofs, but his adversaries had been more embittered than ever. It was his desire now both to express to them the comfort which the news of their submission had brought to him, and also to defend his apostolic authority and personal character against the impugners of both.

It was under these circumstances, and with these objects, that he wrote this Epistle: and with a view of breaking the severity which he was apprehensive of being compelled to employ against the rebellious (see ch. xiii. 10) by, if possible, winning them over before his arrival.

Hardly any of the Epistles is so various in character and style, and so difficult to enter into and ap-

---

* Much of this which immediately follows is taken, with some slight alterations, from the Introduction to my "New Testament for English Readers."

preciate as this:—'consolation and rebuke, gentleness and severity, earnestness and irony; succeed one another at very short intervals, and without notice.'

Meyer remarks: 'The excitement and interchange of the affections, and probably also the haste under which Paul wrote this Epistle, certainly render the expressions often obscure and the constructions difficult: but serve only to exalt our admiration of the great oratorical delicacy, art, and power with which this outpouring of Paul's spirit, especially interesting as a self-defensive apology, flows and streams onward, till at length in the sequel its billows completely overflow the opposition of the adversaries.' Erasmus strikingly says, 'Learned men bestow much toil in explaining the designs of poets and rhetoricians: but in this rhetorician much more toil is required to apprehend what he is about, whither he tends, what it is that he forbids: so full of tortuosities is he, if I may say it without blame. Such is his versatility, that you would hardly think one and the same man was speaking. At one time he wells up gently like some limpid spring; and by-and-by he thunders down like a torrent with a mighty crash, carrying everything with him by the way: now he flows placidly and smoothly, now spreads out far and wide, as if expanded into a lake. Then again in places he disappears and suddenly reappears in some different place, and with wonderful meanders washes now one bank, now the other, and sometimes digressing to a distance, by a backward winding returns upon himself.'

I may add, that of all the considerable epistles in the New Testament, this at first sight, and on our ordinary impression, contains the least matter of great and universal interest to the Christian Church. But first sight, and our ordinary impression, give way upon more mature examination. We shall attempt to show this as we proceed in our summary of the contents. We shall find that even exclusive of the very important passages which here and there meet us, full of weighty revelations and of comfort for all ages of the Church,—in the midst of the personal portions we have continually precious texts of worldwide import occurring.

The Epistle opens with the customary greeting, the Apostle associating with himself Timothy, as he had done Sosthenes in the former letter. This mention of Timothy was opportune here, as we learn from 1 Cor. iv. 17, that he had been sent to

Corinth to 'bring them to remembrance of the Apostle's ways in Christ.' These associations of others with himself, are never allowed to interfere in the least degree with the individuality of the Epistles in which they occur.

And now, from ch. i. 3, at once begin the personal matters which make this Epistle so difficult to explain and put together for us who live at a distance from them. The Apostle speaks of great suffering undergone by him, even to danger of his life (ver. 8), expresses deep thankfulness for his deliverance, and states its purpose to have been that he also might be able to comfort others in tribulation. To what he here alludes is, and must remain, uncertain. One thing we may safely say; that it was not to the peril arising out of the tumult narrated in Acts xix. 'So that we despaired even of life' (ver. 8) is not an expression applicable to danger from a mob, but rather to tedious suffering, which, from minor afflictions, at last threatened even the seat of life. The same may be said of the words 'we had the sentence of death in ourselves,' which look more like a deadly sickness than any danger from without. But, as we said, the matter must remain in obscurity.

But, in thus opening, the Apostle evidently has a further purpose, which soon begins to unfold itself. Chrysostom, with his usual admirable tact, explains as follows :—

'The fact of the Apostle's not coming annoyed and discomposed them, especially as he had promised he would come, but had spent all the time in Macedonia, and seemed to have preferred others to them. For this cause, knowing the feeling against him on this matter, he tells them the cause of his not coming. But he does not set it down plainly, nor does he say, "I know that I promised to come, but as I was hindered by troubles, forgive me, and do not charge me with contempt of you, or fickleness of purpose:" but manages the matter in another way, in a more dignified and trustworthy manner, exalting it by speaking of consolation in his troubles, that they might not even ask for the cause wherefore he disappointed them.'

This postponed journey to Corinth becomes more and more the subject, till in ver. 23 it is openly brought forward. It was to spare them, that he forbore his coming, not from any fickleness of purpose. And he continues in chap. ii. to expound this his reason, referring to the case of the offending person dealt with in 1 Cor. v., and giving directions for the reinstatement of this now penitent offender in the favour of the church. He proceeds to tell them how anxious he had been for the news from Corinth which Titus was to bring; and takes occasion thereby to write (verses 14—17) some golden sentences respecting the dignity, and the duties, of his office.

Continuing this same strain in ch. iii. he draws a contrast-parallel, in allegory, between the Christian and the Jewish ministrations. I may observe in passing, that this passage and that in Gal. iv. 21—31, form striking links between the teaching of St. Paul and that of the writer of the Epistle to the Hebrews, and serve to show that the latter, if not writing under the influence of the Apostle himself, was thoroughly imbued with his spirit, and his mode of allegorising.

The same subject, the apostolic office, and himself as the holder of it, is treated as far as ch. vi. 10. He sets forth his ministerial feelings, sufferings, and hopes, partly with regard to his connection with the Corinthians, but for the most part in general terms. In the midst of this highly personal matter, occurs one of those grand expositions of Christian faith and hope which are the resting-places of believing hearts in all time. It extends from ch. iv. 16 to ch. v. 10. Notice in it—and this will be better done after making the corrections indicated in the latter part of this chapter—how the confident expectation which was expressed in the words, 'we which are alive and remain unto the coming of the Lord,' begins to give way to uncertainty as to whether that day would find the Apostle still clothed with the body, or in the 'unclothed' state. We shall hereafter find it deeply interesting to watch how this very uncertainty itself has given way to the prospect of 'departing and being with Christ' in the later thoughts of the Epistle to the Philippians. Such evidences of a natural change of view on a point which the Lord himself left expressly uncertain, are invaluable as testimonies to the reality and truthfulness of the apostolic Epistles: and more than compensate us, even in outward bulwarks of the faith, for the collapse of the verbal inspiration theory.

But to proceed. From ch. v. 10 to the end of the chapter, the conclusion is drawn which the earlier verses had introduced,—the high and self-denying position of the Christian ministry, and the nature of its work, as a reconciliation of man to God.

This description is further wrought out in ch. vi.; and the earnest pleading with the Corinthians which results from it is carried on into ch. vii. It then gradually passes into an explanatory narrative of his anxiety to receive news of the effect of his former letter, and his heartfelt joy, when he learned how they had felt respecting it.

In ch. viii. he exhorts them to the duty of contributing to the wants of the poor saints at Jerusalem. That metropolis of the church was passing through dark and stormy days: and the peculiar position of the believers there seems to have first given rise to, and then continued, as a feature found in Jerusalem only, that community of goods which we witnessed in the former chapters of the Acts. The common chest of the church at Jerusalem seems to have been replenished by contributions from all the daughter churches: and as yet, though Macedonia in its poverty had been liberal, the flourishing and wealthy Corinthians had proved but backward and scanty in their bestowal. In the course of chapters viii., ix., there are several allusions to circumstances with which we are but imperfectly acquainted: as, for instance, the mission of certain persons, mentioned ch. viii. 18—22, concerning whom it can never be determined, who they were among the companions of the Apostle.

And now, with ch. x., begins the direct personal defence of St. Paul against his rivals and adversaries: and with it, the delicate and intricate alternations of gravity and irony, earnest pleading, and sportive rallying, which make this portion of the Epistle so exceedingly difficult. It is hardly needful to say that the whole of these last four chapters is very precious, both as letting us into the personal character and ways of the Apostle, and as abounding with rich gems of faith, hope, and Christian charity. The description of his practice in ch. x., the narrative of his perils in ch. xi., the mysterious passage about his visions and revelations in ch. xii., with the answer of the Lord to his troubled prayer, are portions which we feel to be indispensable to our thorough knowledge of St. Paul and his work, and by consequence, of the whole primitive system and age of Christianity. The last chapter contains a grave declaration of his resolution to come among them, and exhortations and denunciations, grounded on the certainty of that his approaching visit. The final salutation is cut off very short, in accordance with the serious and almost minatory tone of this conclusion; and the letter ends with that benediction in the express name of the Holy Trinity, which has become the accustomed formula of dismissal throughout the ages of the Christian Church.

We now come to our usual task of correcting places in which our translators have either used a faulty text, or have insufficiently rendered the text which they had before them. And first, for the places in which the text used by our translators is not that of the oldest and best authorities.

In chap. i. 6, the verse should stand thus:— 'But whether we be in tribulation, it is for your comfort and salvation, which worketh in the endurance of the same sufferings which we also suffer (and our hope is steadfast for you): or whether we be comforted, it is for your comfort and salvation.' Then the next verse begins, 'knowing that as ye are,' &c. In ver. 10, '*doth* deliver' should stand 'will deliver.' In ver. 12, instead of '*simplicity*,' all our most ancient MSS. have 'holiness.' In the Greek, the words are much alike: 'simplicity' being *haplotés*, 'holiness,' *hagiotés*. In ver. 18, for '*was* not' we should read 'is not.' Ver. 20 should be read and rendered, 'For how many soever be the promises of God, in Him is the yea: wherefore through Him is the Amen, for glory unto God by us.'

In ch. ii. 10, '*for if I forgave anything, to whom I forgave it,*' read 'for indeed what I have forgiven, if I have forgiven anything.'

In ch. iv. 1, instead of 'we faint not,' most of the oldest MSS. have 'we shrink not back.' The difference in the Greek is only that of one letter—'we faint' being '*ekkakoumen;*' 'we shrink,' '*enkakoumen.*' In ver. 6, for '*commanded the light to shine out of darkness,*' read, 'said out of darkness light shall shine.' In ver. 10, '*the Lord*' should be omitted. In ver. 14, '*by* Jesus,' should be 'with Jesus.' In ver. 16, 'faint not' should be 'shrink not back;' see on ver. 1.

Chap. v. 5, omit '*also.*' Ver. 12, omit, '*for.*' Ver. 14, for '*that if one died for all, then were all dead,*' read 'that one died for all, therefore all died.' In ver. 17, for '*all things* are become new,' read 'they are become new.' In ver. 18, omit '*Jesus.*' In ver. 21, omit '*For.*'

In ch. vii. 12, for '*our care for you,*' read and render 'your earnest care for us.' Ver. 13 should stand, 'For this cause we have been comforted' but in our comfort we joyed the more exceedingly for the joy of Titus,' &c.

Chap. viii. 4, should stand, 'praying of us with much intreaty the grace and the participation in the ministering unto the saints.' In ver. 12, for '*that a man hath*,' read 'that which it (viz., the willing mind) may have.' In ver. 19, for '*to the glory of the same Lord, and declaration of your ready mind*,' read 'to the glory of the Lord, and the furtherance of our zeal.' In ver. 21, instead of 'providing,' read 'for we provide.'

In ch. ix. 4, '*in this same confident boasting*,' should be 'in this same confidence.' In ver. 5, for '*your bounty, whereof ye had notice before*,' read 'your promised blessing.' In ver. 10, '*minister . . . multiply . . . increase*,' should be 'shall minister . . . shall multiply . . . shall increase.' It is not a wish, but a prophetic assertion.

In ch. x. 7, the word '*Christ's*,' the second time it occurs, should be omitted. It, of course, may be supplied in the sense; but it does not exist in the ancient text. The same may be said of '*us*' in ver. 8, which though fairly supplied in the sense, is not in the ancient text.

Chap. xi. 3, for '*the simplicity that is in Christ,*

read 'the simplicity and the purity that is toward Christ.' In ver. 4, for '*ye might well bear with him,*' read 'ye with reason bear with him.' In ver. 6, for '*we have been throughly made manifest among you in all things,*' read 'in everything did we make things manifest unto you before all men.' In ver. 10, for '*no man shall stop me of this boasting,*' read 'this boasting shall not be shut against me.' In ver. 28, for '*that which cometh upon me daily,*' read 'my care day by day.' In ver. 32, omit '*desirous.*'

In ch. xii. 1, the readings are in great confusion. That which seems to claim the preference is, 'I must needs boast, though it is not expedient.' In ver. 3, for '*out of,*' read 'apart from.' In ver. 9, it is uncertain whether we ought to retain '*my*' (before 'strength') in the text. In ver. 11, omit '*in glorying.*' In ver. 19, for '*again, think ye that we excuse ourselves unto you?*' ought to stand 'ye have been long thinking that we are excusing ourselves unto you.'

Chap. xiii. 2, ought to stand 'I have said already, and now say beforehand, as when I was present the second time, so now also in my absence, to them which,' &c. In ver. 4, '*for though He was crucified*,' ought to be 'for indeed He was crucified.' Ver. 7 ought to begin 'Yet we pray,' instead of '*Now, I pray.*' The '*Amen*' at the end is an addition not found in any of the most ancient MSS.

The list of mistaken and imperfect renderings in this Epistle is far larger. There is hardly any, where the translators have more frequently failed to catch the sense, or to represent the connection. And in consequence, many parts of it fall heavy and flat on the ear of the English reader. The delicate turns of the Apostle's courtesy mixed with severity, the keenness of his exquisite irony, the playfulness of his half suppressed allusions, have been rudely disguised, or lost, in the hands of King James's divines.

In ch. i. 5, '*in* us' is a misrendering. It should be 'unto us;' and '*by* Christ' should be 'through Christ.' In ver. 9, '*have had*' should be 'had.' In ver. 12, for 'not *with* fleshly wisdom but *by* the grace of God,' render, 'not in fleshly wisdom but in the grace of God.' In ver. 14, for '*rejoicing*' should stand 'boast.' In verses 21 and 22, omit 'hath' twice. In ver. 23, for '*record*' read 'witness.'

Chap. ii. ver. 5 is one of those cases where the delicacy of the Apostle's blame has been obliterated by the translators. What he says, is this, that the offender has not wronged *him*, but in a measure (he will not say this without qualification, lest he bear too hardly on him) all of them—the whole Corinthian church. This meaning would be expressed thus: 'But if any hath caused sorrow, he hath not caused sorrow to me, but in part (that I press not too heavily) to you all.' This is completely disguised by our present version, '*he hath not grieved me, but in part: that I may not overcharge you all.*' In ver. 12, '*to preach* the Gospel of Christ' should be 'for the Gospel of Christ;' there is nothing about *preaching* in the original. In ver. 14, '*causeth us to triumph*' seems to be a misrendering. The verb implies to 'lead in triumph,' *i. e.* to 'triumph over;' and the meaning seems to be, that God ceases not to exhibit us, his former foes, as overcome by Him. The literal rendering, which would carry this meaning, would be 'leadeth us in triumph.' The 'sweet savour' spoken of immediately after is in pursuance of the same figure: as during a triumph sweet spices were thrown about, or burnt in the streets.

In ch. iii. 6, 'who *hath made us able ministers*' gives a wrong idea; it should be, 'who hath enabled us as ministers,' 'given us power to become ministers,' or 'made us sufficient as ministers,' keeping the same expression as has been used before. In ver. 13, '*could* not' should be 'might not.' The Apostle is speaking, not of a result, but of a purpose. This whole passage is commonly misunderstood, by reason of a mistake in our version of Exod. xxxiv. 35. It is commonly assumed that Moses *spoke* to the Israelites, *having the vail on his face;* and this is implied in our version—'till Moses had done speaking with them, he put a vail on his face.' But the Hebrew and Septuagint give a different account : 'and *when he ceased speaking* to them, he put a vail over his face.' He spoke to them *without* the vail, with his face shining and glorified :—*when he had done speaking*, he placed the vail on his face : and that, not because they were afraid to look on him, but as here, *that they might not look on the end*, or the fading, *of that transitory glory :* that they might only see it as long as it was the credential of his ministry, and then it might be withdrawn from their eyes. Thus the declaration of God's will to them was not in openness of speech, but was interrupted and broken by intervals of concealment, which ours is not. In ver. 14, the words ought to stand 'at the reading of the Old Testament the same vail remaineth, it not being discovered that it is done away in Christ.' In ver. 17, '*that* Spirit' should be 'the Spirit.' In ver. 18, '*open*,' which drops the similitude, should be 'unvailed.' The vail was removed at our conversion. At the end of the verse is a flagrant mistranslation, again obscuring the sense. The words thus rendered cannot by any possibility mean '*the Spirit of the Lord*:' they may be rendered in two or three ways, but not in this. By far the best is, 'the Lord the Spirit;' the Lord, who, it had been said in ver. 17, 'is the Spirit.'

In ch. iv. 3, where the same image of the vail is again recurred to, the translators, with singular infelicity, have managed to obliterate it. It ought to stand, 'And even if our Gospel is vailed, it is vailed to them that are perishing.' In the same verse, '*the glorious Gospel*' should be 'Gospel of the glory': the good news of the glory of Christ. Verse 15 is a difficult verse. The most probable rendering is this, 'That grace, being multiplied by means of the greater number, may make the thanksgiving abound unto the glory of God.' In ver. 17, '*our light affliction which is but for a moment*,' would be, more correctly, 'our present light affliction.' In ver. 18, '*temporal*' should be 'for a time.' It is not the worldly or secular character but the fleeting nature of the things that are seen, which the Apostle is setting forth.

Chap. v. has been lamentably disguised in the rendering: the fineness of fancy displayed in the imagery obliterated, and the meaning confused. The corrections can hardly be made except by giving a totally different English text. Still, we must try. In ver. 1, '*house of this tabernacle*' should be 'tabernacle wherein we dwell.' The introduction of the word '*house*' here, sadly mars the imagery. The Apostle was a *tent*-maker; and the tents were made of the Cilician haircloth, which was also used for *clothing*. Hence the mingling of the images of dwelling and clothing, which in our version is unintelligible, because we do not wear the materials of which houses are built. '*Of God*,' should be 'from God.' And after '*eternal*,' a comma should be placed.* In ver. 2,

---

* This has been omitted in the text of my "New Testament for English Readers," though implied in the note.

for '*earnestly desiring to be clothed upon*,' write 'longing to clothe ourselves.' The English version involves a blunder in the *voice* of the Greek verb. Ver. 3 should stand 'seeing that we shall verily be found clothed, and not naked.' The verse asserts strongly, with a view to substantiate and explain ver. 2, the truth of the resurrection in a glorified body, probably in reference to the deniers of the resurrection at Corinth: and the sense is 'For I do assert again, that we shall in that day prove to be clothed with a body, and not disembodied spirits.' In ver. 6, the full sense of the words would be better given by 'whilst we are in our home in the body, we are away from our home in the Lord.' In the parenthesis which follows 'not by *sight*' should be 'not by appearance.' The word signifies not that *by which* we see, but that *which* we see. Again, we should express it, 'to go from our home in the body, and to come to our home with the Lord.' In ver. 10, '*appear*' ought to be, 'be made manifest.' Ver. 11, is a curious instance of mis-rendering: and is often used and preached upon as having a sense which was never in the Apostle's mind. His meaning is, 'knowing then,' being ourselves conscious of, 'the fear of the Lord,' *i. e.*, being God-fearing persons ourselves, looking for, and living under the consciousness of, this éclaircissement before Christ's judgment-seat—'we persuade MEN,' *i. e.*, it is MEN that we attempt to persuade, not God, to whom we are already made manifest. The '*terror*,' or '*terrors*,' as sometimes further misquoted, has been altogether imported into the verse: and the excellent lesson so often preached from it, that being aware of the terrible judgments of God, we *persuade* others to avoid them, is wholly alien from its purport. In ver. 13. '*to God*' should be 'for God.' In ver. 14, '*the love of Christ*' should have been expressed 'Christ's love.' It is not our love to Christ, but His to us which is spoken of. '*The love of Christ*' may mean this, but is ambiguous. '*Then all were dead*' is a sad misrendering and obscuration of the sense. It should be 'then all died.' It does not follow, because one dies for another, that that other *was dead*, but it does follow that that other *died* by substitution, virtually died, inasmuch as one died *for him*. And thus we all died in Christ's death *for us*. In ver. 18, omit '*hath*' twice. In ver. 19, the words should stand, 'to wit, that God was reconciling the world unto Himself in Christ.' Again, omit '*hath*.'

In ver. 20, omit '*you.*' It is the general office of the ministry of which he is speaking.

In chap. vi., from the beginning of ver. 6 to the word 'God' in ver. 7, the prepositions should all be 'in:' and then to the end of the list in ver. 8, 'through.' The Apostle having made this difference, the translators ought to have carefully observed it, instead of rendering both the Greek words by an indiscriminate 'by.'

In chap. vii. 2, omit 'have' three times. Ver. 13 should stand 'For this cause we have been comforted; but in our comfort we joyed the more exceedingly,' &c. In ver. 14, '*I am not ashamed*' ought to be 'I was not put to shame:' and '*is found*,' 'was found.'

In chap. viii. 1, 'make known to you' would now be better understood than the obsolete '*do you to wit of.*' In ver. 16, '*put*' should be 'putteth.' In ver. 22, '*I have*,' supplied by the translators, should be 'he hath.' In ver. 23, '*the messengers*' should have been faithfully rendered as St. Paul wrote it, 'Apostles.' A mere ecclesiastical difficulty should not induce us to quash the weighty testimony of a word like this being used of other persons than those commonly thus known. There is no definite article before 'Apostles.'

Chap. ix. 4. '*they of Macedonia*' should be 'any Macedonians.' In ver. 5, '*bounty*' (twice) ought to be 'blessing': and in the next verse '*bountifully*' should be 'with blessings.'

Chap. xi. 1, '*and indeed bear with me*' ought to be 'but indeed ye do bear with me.' In ver. 4, for '*preacheth*' and '*receive*,' read 'as preaching,' and 'are receiving.' He is supposing a fact, not merely stating a contingency. And in the same verse, for '*have not preached*' and '*have not accepted*,' read 'preached not' and 'accepted not.' In the next verse, for '*the very chiefest apostles*' should stand 'those overmuch apostles :' *i. e.*, those men who pretend to be more than the Apostles themselves. He means, the false and rival teachers, not the Apostles. This, which I have endeavoured to substantiate in my note on the passage, is clear from the context in which the same expression occurs, ch. xii. 11 (see below). In ver. 16 'I' should be 'I too,' viz., as well as they. In ver. 21 the words should stand, 'By way of disparagement I assume that we were weak,' thus ironically calling to mind his abstinence, when among them, from all these acts of self-exaltation at their expense. In ver. 28, for '*the care of,*' read 'my anxiety for.'

In ch. xii. 2, 'I *knew* a man,' should be 'I know a man.' This is a serious blunder. The Apostle is not speaking of one whom he once, but of one whom he now knows. Fourteen years ago is the date, not of the *knowledge*, as our version makes it, but of the *vision*. The same is the case in ver. 3 also. At the end of ver. 6, '*of* me' should be 'from me.' In ver. 7, for '*the messenger,*' 'the angel.' There was no reason for departing from the ordinary New Testament meaning of the word. In ver. 8, '*for*' would be better 'concerning.' In ver. 11, for '*am* I behind,' read 'came I behind.' The translators have knowingly misrendered the past tense to suit their sense. For 'the *very chiefest Apostles,*' read as above, 'those overmuch Apostles.' This is absolutely required here. St. Paul challenges them to compare him with his rivals among them, and states that in no particular did he come behind them. This could not apply to the Twelve, whom the Corinthians had never seen. The translators were aware of this, and in bad faith altered the past tense, 'came I behind,' to a present, '*am* I behind.' This is the way the word of God has been dealt with in a version vaunted as perfect and verbally inspired. In ver. 15, for 'you' should stand 'your souls.' The words are plain in the original, and why the translators changed them must be ever a mystery.

Chap. xiii. 9, '*wish*' should be 'pray for.' Ver. 11, '*farewell*' should be 'rejoice,' viz., in the Lord.

VI.

THE EPISTLE TO THE GALATIANS.

IT is hardly possible to imagine a letter surpassing this in interest or in marked character. Those to whom it was written, the occasion which gave birth to it, the strong personal feelings and convictions of the writer—these are all before us in marked and unmistakable outlines. We shall endeavour to present each in turn before our readers.

The Galatians, or Gauls, or Kelts, for the name is probably but one and the same under these different forms, are found at the earliest historic period inhabiting the greater part of Western Europe. When we first encounter them, they are a restless, migratory people, making incursions on their neighbours, and occupying new territories by conquest. In the fourth century before Christ, we see Rome itself sacked and plundered by them; shortly after, the famous temple at Delphi suffers their attack and witnesses their repulse. A detachment of this same invading body wandered away into the far east, and overran the lesser Asia. There eventually, after a series of vicissitudes, which it is beside our purpose to relate, they became settled. The central portion of Asia Minor, known as Galatia, was their country; and at the time of the apostolic history, gave its name to, and was itself part of, a Roman province, slightly exceeding its own extent. Mingled with this invading people were a considerable number of the original Phrygian inhabitants; and, what is more important for our present purpose, a large and influential Jewish element.

Still, the character of the population in the main was that of the Gauls or Kelts. Its description by independent writers is full of interest for the readers of this Epistle. Cæsar, the great conqueror of Gaul, describes himself as taking certain precautions, 'fearing the weakness of the Gauls, because they are fickle in taking up plans, and ever fond of innovating, and therefore he thought that no trust should be put in them.' The his-

torian of the Gauls, Thierry, thus describes them:
—'They have a frank, impetuous spirit, open to every impression, intelligent in the extreme: but with all this, excessive mobility, a total want of constancy, abundance of ostentation, and lastly a perpetual tendency to quarrel, arising from excessive vanity.' The Roman historian Livy says that they were physically unable to bear endurance in toil or heat; and that from this circumstance, coupled with their excitable ardour, at the beginning of their battles they were almost stronger than men, at the end of them weaker than women.

Professor Lightfoot, in the Introduction to his admirable work on this Epistle, gives some other interesting traits of Celtic character to which possibly allusions may be traced in it:—

'St. Paul's language will suggest many coincidences which perhaps we are tempted to press unduly. His denunciation of "drunkenness and revelling" (chap. v. 21), falling in with the taunts of ancient writers, will appear to point to a darling sin of the Celtic people. His condemnation of the niggardly spirit with which they had doled out their alms, as a "mockery of God" (chap. vi. 6, 7), will remind us that the race is constantly reproached with its greed of wealth, so that Gaulish avarice has passed almost into a proverb. His reiterated warning against strife and vain-glory (chap. v. 15, 26: compare v. 20, 21; vi. 3), will seem directed against a vice of the old Celtic blood still boiling in their veins, and breaking out in fierce and rancorous self-assertion. His very expression, "if ye bite and devour one another," will recall the angry gesticulations and menacing tones of this irritable people.'

But the main feature of their character with which we are in this Epistle concerned, is their restless love of change. They had received the Gospel at the hands of St. Paul, with their usual fervour and impetuosity. But at the time of his writing this letter, they were rapidly changing to another gospel, which was not another (chap. i. 6): and the nature of that change is not without its interest. It was being brought about by Jewish influence, and was in the direction of the Mosaic rites and ceremonies. Now Cæsar's description of the Gauls is, that they are above all other people given to superstitious observances; so that here again we have a point of national character brought out.

We proceed to give an account of St. Paul's connection with this remarkable people. In Acts xvi. 6, we read that the Apostle, who had, in company with Silas, revisited the churches previously founded by him in Lycaonia, 'went through the Phrygian and Galatian country:'—for so the words should be read. No more is here said. It would appear from Gal. iv. 3, that his intention had been merely to pass through, but that he was detained by a sickness. (See below the correction of reading in this passage.) What sickness that was, is no matter of doubt; for the same passage contains a distinct allusion to his constitutional infirmity, his 'thorn in the flesh' (2 Cor. xii.), whatever that may have been. He appears to have taken occasion by this detention to preach to them the Gospel; and to found the Galatian churches, of which churches we have no particular account.

His description of the reception which they gave to his message is in accordance with their fervent national temperament. They took no account of the temptation in his flesh, which made him appear contemptible; they received him as an angel of God, nay, as if he had been our Lord himself. In an expression which must ever remain somewhat obscure, but which testifies to the exaggerated nature of their affectionate excitement, they were ready to have plucked out their own eyes and have given them to him, in the self-congratulations which they expressed at his being among them (chap. iv. 14, 15).

But this was not his only visit. We find him in Acts xviii. 23, carrying out a more formal visitation: going through the whole country in order, confirming all the disciples. This was after an interval of at least three years; and it is to this second visit that some allusions of an instructive character, occurring in the Epistle, must be referred. In chap. iv. 16, he asks them reproachingly, whether *he had become their enemy by telling them the truth?* These words cannot of course apply to that first visit; as little can they be interpreted of anything in the Epistle, which the Galatians had not yet received; but their reference must be found in something that happened on the second presence of the Apostle among them. Then he must have found the evil beginning to be apparent, and have spoken to them his mind about it. Some hints are given of the character of his plain-spoken warnings. In chap. i. 9, he says,

'As *we said before*, so now I say again, If any man preacheth unto you any other gospel than that which ye received, let him be accursed.' The perverters of the Gospel had already begun their teaching; they were preaching conformity to the Jewish law; for he says, chap. v. 3, 'I testify *again* to every man that is circumcised, that he is a debtor to do the whole law.' This also had formed a portion of his warning at the second visit. But matters were even worse than this. In chap. v. 21, having enumerated the works of the flesh, he adds, ' of the which I forewarn you, *as I also forewarned you before*, that they who do such things shall not inherit the kingdom of God.'

After this second visit, the Apostle remained a considerable time—*three years*, as he himself calls it, Acts xx. 31—at Ephesus. There he would hear frequently of the progress of error among the Galatian churches; thence we know that he sent to them an order to contribute for the help of the poor brethren at Jerusalem (1 Cor. xvi. 1—6). A very general opinion has been, that this Epistle was written during the stay at Ephesus. The expression in chap. i. 6, 'I marvel that ye are *so soon* removing from Him that called you,' seems hardly to allow of a longer interval than three years having elapsed since that calling took place. Still, this is not the only consideration to be taken into account. The Epistles of St. Paul form themselves naturally into various groups, each of which is pervaded by a similar spirit and tone of the Apostle's mind, not found to prevail in others. We shall have occasion hereafter to follow out this idea in more instances than one. At present, let us bear it in mind while comparing 2 Corinthians, Galatians, and Romans. It cannot be denied that remarkable affinities bind together these three Epistles. The necessity of self-vindication, existing with regard to both churches, causes the personal portions of 2 Corinthians and Galatians to have much in common. Very differently, it is true, does the Apostle shape his 'apology' to the two churches. The great hard lines of his vigorous self-assertion to the Galatians are softened into delicate and subtle irony of compliment to the Corinthians. But the same anxiety for his influence and office as bound up with the declaration of Christ's truth, causes the same spirit, in spite of the differing vehicle, to pervade both Epistles, and binds them inseparably together as works of the same period. Still more strikingly is our Epistle united to the Epistle to the Romans. Whole passages, consisting of arguments on the relation of Christians to the law and its ordinances, are almost identical in the two. Compare together Gal. iii. 6—29 and Rom. iv. 3, 10, 11, 17, 18, i. 17, x. 5, xi. 32, vi. 3, and xiii. 14; Gal. iv. 5—7 and Rom. viii. 14—17; Gal. ii. 16 and Rom. iii. 20; Gal. v. 14 and Rom. xiii. 8—10; ver. 16 and Rom. viii. 4; ver. 17 and Rom. vii. 15, 23, 25; and many other passages and expressions. As Professor Lightfoot has remarked, 'there is no parallel to this close resemblance in St. Paul's Epistles, except in the case of the letters to the Colossians and Ephesians. Those letters were written about the same time and sent by the same messenger, and I cannot but think that we should be doing violence to historic probability by separating the Epistles to the Galatians and Romans from each other by an interval of more than a few months.' He finds a common link between the three Epistles, serving to place this one intermediate between the two others, in the lists of sins, 2 Cor. xii. 20, 21; Gal. v. 19—21; Rom. xiii. 13.

If we adopt this view, then St. Paul must have

written the Epistle from Corinth, during his stay there after he had written the second Epistle to the Corinthians in Macedonia; or perhaps partly in Macedonia on his journey, and partly after his arrival at Corinth. Professor Lightfoot gives several other reasons, grounded on St. Paul's way of speaking of his personal sufferings in the three Epistles, his doctrinal statements, the progress of opposition to him on the part of the Jews, and his mode of treating offenders, why this order of the three, rather than the commonly-supposed one should be adopted. And I own, though this was not always my opinion, that I am now disposed to think with him.

When we come to speak of the character of this Epistle, our task is an easy one. It is indeed marked and unmistakable from the first. The letter sprung out of two circumstances, both belonging to the same growing apostasy on the part of the Galatians. They were falling from the gospel of the grace of Christ, and they were repudiating his apostolic authority. On this their twofold fault the whole Epistle is the comment. First of all, after denouncing in the plainest terms their fickleness, he proceeds to defend the apostolic character of his ministry, and its independence on human testimony. This he does by giving a history of his intercourse with the other Apostles at and after his own conversion: ending with a remarkable account of an occasion at Antioch when he found himself compelled to withstand and openly rebuke St. Peter. The value to the Church of this narration cannot be over-esteemed. It has set before us the reality of the conflicts of the apostolic Church, and the fallibility of the great leaders of it, in a way for which we cannot be too thankful. It is hardly strange that, in the midst of the superstition which has ever clung to the estimate of the Apostles' character and work, this very passage itself should have been made a subject of contention. Jerome, with that want of ingenuousness which he so often shows, endeavoured to explain it away, and to make out that there was no difference between the Apostles after all. Whereupon Augustine, the most honest, as he was far the most able, of the Fathers, wrote to him most plainly and seriously, warning him of the consequences to the cause of truth, if such an explanation were allowed to stand. It is much to Jerome's credit, that he openly retracted his dishonest interpretation.

At chap. iii. the polemical portion at once begins, with that abruptness and fervour which are the characteristics of our Epistle. Who had bewitched and seduced them into such folly as they were now showing? They had *seen* Christ crucified, in the Apostle's plain setting of Him forth: but some one had raised a counter-spell, had obscured and drawn them away from that holy vision. They had begun in a high and glorious spiritual course: they were seeking to be perfected in a low, beggarly, carnal one. Not so Abraham, the father of the faithful, who was justified by faith, and whose children walk by faith and are blessed. The law brings not blessing, but a curse; from which curse Christ hath delivered us. And God's covenant of faith with Abraham, ratified long before the law, could never be set aside nor modified by that subsequent dispensation which was merely interposed for a temporary purpose, and that purpose, fulfilled when Christ came, clothing us with the fulness of our adoption as sons in God's family.

Here (chap. iv. 8) he again turns abruptly to the Galatians, and breaks out into fervid, but at the same time most affectionate pleading with them on their strange conduct as regarded the Gospel and himself: recounting the totally different reception given by them to both on his first visit amongst them.

And now follows a remarkable passage, in which St. Paul carries on his argument against the Judaizers by maintaining against them the allegorical sense of that law of which they professed themselves the upholders: by maintaining, that is, that the events, and even the names, which come before us in the Old Testament history, have beneath them spiritual meanings, and are parables of Christian truths. He adopted the same strain in 1 Cor. x., when he spoke of the mystical meaning of the history of the Jews in the wilderness: the same again in 1 Cor. xv., when he insisted on the mutual relations of Adam and of Christ. Mr. Conybeare has well remarked, 'The lesson to be drawn from this whole passage as regards the Christian use of the Old Testament, is of an importance which can scarcely be over-rated.'

The result of the argument from the allegorical interpretation is, that we are not children of a system of bondage, but of liberty wherewith Christ made us free. In this liberty we must stand fast, and not be entangled again in slavery. If we are, Christ has become of no use to us. The adoption of any requirement of the law cuts off from Christ. Who could have perverted the favourable course in which they were once running? Whoever he were, he should bear his punishment. One form of his yearning for the excision of their perverters the Apostle signifies in a wish, which modern language is obliged to veil, but which is all the more characteristic of his burning and irrepressible zeal for the purity of the faith.

And now comes in the third or hortatory portion of the Epistle, by which it appears that, besides fickleness in matter of belief and ceremonial, grave moral faults had broken out among the Galatians: bitter mutual dissension, and licentious following of the lusts of the flesh.

After this, he draws to a close. And that close is as remarkable as the opening. Contrary to his usual practice, he had written this whole letter to them with his own hand: and he directs their attention (see chap. vi. 11, in the corrections below) to the great sprawling handwriting, the consequence probably of his weakness of sight, or unsteadiness of hand, testifying to the earnestness of his all-absorbing feeling for their good. Once more, before ending, he sums up all. It was not for the sake of keeping the law that these troublers were seeking them; but simply that they might boast of them as their own followers. Boast of them? What did he, Paul, feel in his inmost heart about boasting? This, this only: that there is but one thing in the world worth boasting in, the Cross of Christ. In that, was his victory over the world; in that, the world's contempt of him. The newness of life thus brought in is the only thing that avails under the Gospel. All who thus believe and thus live—God bless them, and bless His own Israel in the Spirit! As for him, let none trouble him, for he was the branded slave of Jesus Christ, not his own, but with the marks of his Master upon him. And so, with his prayer for Christ's grace in their spirits, he leaves them.

We have to subjoin our usual list of corrections of reading and rendering. The principal places in which our authorized text differs from that established by the best and most ancient MSS., are the following :—

In chap. i. 10, the second '*for*' should be omitted. In verse 15, for '*it pleased God, who,*' it should stand, 'He pleased, who.'* In verse 17, '*went up*,' and '*went*,' should probably be, both times, 'went away.' The expression conveys, the first time, somewhat of scorn: 'I did not go *wandering away* to seek human intercourse:' and the second time expresses the contrast to this wandering away: 'I went into seclusion.' In verse 18, '*Peter*' should be 'Cephas.'

In ch. ii. 11, '*Peter*' should be 'Cephas,' as also in verse 14: where '*Why compellest thou*' ought to be, 'how is it that thou compellest?' In verse 16, after 'knowing,' insert 'nevertheless.'

In ch. iii. 1, the words '*that ye should not obey the truth*,' should be omitted. They have apparently come in from ch. v. 7, and are not found in the oldest MSS. The words '*among you*' should also be omitted. In ver. 17, the words '*in Christ*' should be omitted; and in ver. 29, 'heirs according to promise' should be read without 'and' preceding.

In ch. iv. 6, '*your* hearts' should be 'our hearts.' In ver. 7, for '*an heir of God through Christ*,' should stand 'an heir through God.' In

---

* This correction has been inadvertently overlooked in my "New Testament for English readers."

ver. 8, '*them which by nature are no gods*,' should be 'gods which by nature exist not.' In ver. 14, for '*my* temptation,' read 'your temptation.' In ver. 24, for '*the* two covenants,' it should be 'two covenants.' The article is wanting in all our MSS., both ancient and later. In ver. 26, for '*the mother of us all*,' read 'our mother.' In ver. 28, many ancient MSS. for 'we,' read 'ye;' but it is not quite clear which should be adopted.

In ch. v. 1, there is considerable confusion of readings. The most probable seems, 'With (or, in) liberty Christ made us free. Stand fast, therefore.' In ver. 19, omit 'adultery.' In ver. 24, for '*Christ's*,' read 'Jesus Christ's.' In ch. vi. 15, '*availeth*,' ought to be 'is.' In ver. 17, '*the Lord Jesus*,' ought to be 'Jesus.'*

The principal corrections to be made in the rendering of the original text by our translators, are the following:—

In ch. i. 6, '*removed*,' ought to be 'removing.' In ver. 8, '*have* prevailed,' should be 'prevailed.' In ver. 9, '*said*,' should be 'have said.' In ver.

---

* In my "New Testament for English Readers," the note stating this omission is, by mistake, printed against the words, 'our Lord,' in ver. 18.

15, '*separated me*,' which is ambiguous, should be 'set me apart.'

In ch. ii. 2, '*I should run, or had run*,' ought to be 'I should be running, or have run.' In ver. 4, '*false brethren*,' should be 'the false brethren.' In ver. 6, '*seemed*,' ought to be 'seem.' He is speaking of the reputation which the other apostles held among the Galatians at the time when he was writing, not at the time when he was in Jerusalem. The same applies to the same word '*seemed*,' in ver. 9, which ought to be 'seem.' (I am indebted for this correction to Professor Lightfoot.) In ver. 8, '*in* Peter,' should be 'for Peter;' and '*in* me,' 'for me.' In ver. 9, '*heathen*,' should be 'Gentiles.' In ver. 11, '*to be blamed*,' should be 'condemned.' Peter was not *to be* blamed, but (in the original it is simply the perfect participle passive) was already by his conduct a condemned man. In ver. 13, '*dissembled likewise with him*,' substitute 'also joined in his hypocrisy;' and at the end of the verse, for '*dissimulation*,' render 'hypocrisy.' In ver. 15, for 'we *who* are,' render 'we are.' In ver. 16, for '*but by*,' render 'save only through;' and for '*the faith of*,' 'faith in;' and for '*even we have believed*,' 'we also believed.'

In ver. 18, for '*make*,' render 'prove.' In ver. 19, for '*are dead*,' substitute 'died.' In ver. 20, for '*am* crucified,' substitute 'have been crucified.' The following clause should stand :—'And it is no longer I that live, but Christ that liveth in me.' In ver. 20, for '*by* the faith,' substitute 'in the faith.' In ver. 21, for '*is* dead in vain,' render 'died without cause.'

In ch. iii. 1, '*hath been* evidently set forth' should be 'was evidently set forth,' viz., when the Apostle was among them. In ver. 3, '*made perfect*' should be 'being made perfect:' it is a present tense, not a past one. In ver. 4, '*Have ye suffered*' should be 'Did ye suffer.' In ver. 5, '*among* you' should be 'in you.' In ver. 7, for '*the children*' render 'sons.' In ver. 8, '*the heathen*,' and '*nations*,' should both be 'Gentiles.' In the same verse, the expression '*preached before the Gospel*' is ambiguous : '*before*' may be either a preposition, 'preached—before the Gospel—unto Abraham,' or an adverb, 'preached before—the Gospel—unto Abraham.' It *is* an *adverb*, and the ambiguity should be removed by substituting 'beforehand,' which gives the meaning unmistakably. In ver. 11, the words '*the just shall live by faith*' ought to stand, 'the just by faith (*i.e.* they that are justified by faith) shall live.' The stress of the argument here is on the contrast between those that are just by faith, and those whose righteousness arises from having done the works of the law: the attainment of *life* being common to both. In ver. 12, '*doeth*' should be 'hath done.' In ver. 13, '*hath* redeemed' should be 'redeemed.' In ver. 14, '*through*' should be 'in.' In ver. 15, '*yet if it be confirmed*' should be 'when it hath been ratified.' In ver. 17, '*cannot*' should be 'doth not.' In ver. 18, '*gave*' should be 'hath given.' In ver. 19, '*was made*' should be 'is made.' Ver. 20 would be clearer expressed, 'Now a mediator cannot be of one (*i.e.* necessarily requires two parties), but God is one' (one in Himself, and essentially one in His purposes and actions). In ver. 21, for '*should*,' render 'would.' In ver. 22, '*hath concluded*' should be 'concluded,' or better ' shut up.' In ver. 24, '*was*' should be 'hath become;' and '*might*' should be 'may.' In ver. 25, '*after that faith is come*' should be 'now that faith is come.' Verses 26 and 27 should stand thus : ' For ye are all sons of God through the faith in Christ

Jesus. For all ye who were baptized into Christ did put on Christ.' In ver. 28, 'Ye are all *one*' would be more correctly and clearly expressed, 'Ye are all one man.' The word '*one*' in the original is masculine; and it is the unity of all mankind in the manhood of Christ that the Apostle is insisting on. In ver. 29, for '*the* promise' should stand 'promise.'

In ch. iv. 2, 'tutors and governors' would be more correctly expressed 'guardians and stewards;' and in ver. 3, 'rudiments' would be nearer the sense than 'elements;' as also in v. 9. In this latter verse, '*now after that ye have known God*, should be 'now that ye know God.' In the end of the verse, 'again' does not sufficiently express the meaning, which is 'again from the beginning.' In ver. 12, '*ye have not injured me at all*' should be 'ye did me no wrong.' In ver. 13, '*through infirmity of the flesh,*' should be 'because of an infirmity of my flesh.' It was an illness which first detained him in Galatia : see the introduction to this chapter. In ver. 17, '*affect*' does not convey much meaning to the modern reader : 'court' would express the sense better. The same applies to the next verse; where also 'in a good cause' would be better than 'in a good thing.' In ver. 22, for '*a*' (twice), read 'the.' In ver. 23, for '*promise*,' 'the promise.' In ver. 24, for '*are an allegory*,' 'have another meaning.' In ver. 25, for '*this Agar is Mount Sinai in Arabia*,' read 'the word Hagar is in Arabia (*i.e.* in the Arabic language) Mount Sinai;' which appears to have been the case. The Chaldee paraphrast of the Old Testament uses it with this meaning. In ver. 31, '*the* bondwoman' should be 'a bondwoman:' 'we are not children of any bondmaid, but of *the* (the chosen, the well-known) freewoman.'

In ch. v. 12, it is not possible to present to the English reader the Apostle's meaning in plain words. I can only refer to what was said above, in treating of the contents of the Epistle. It may suffice to say that the authorised version does not in the least degree represent his wish: and to refer to my New Testament for English Readers, or my Greek Testament, for further explanation. In ver. 13, '*have been called*,' should be 'were called.' In ver. 17, '*so that ye cannot*' ought to be, 'that ye may not.' In ver 19, '*which are these*' should be 'such as.' Those which follow are not all the works of the flesh, but merely specimens of them.

In ch. vi. 6, '*communicate unto*' ought to be 'share with.' In ver. 11, how 'large a letter' ought to have been rendered 'in how large letters.' He is speaking not of the length of the Epistle, but of the great coarse handwriting, testifying that he wrote it with his own hand.

VII.

THE EPISTLE TO THE ROMANS.

(*First Part.*)

WE have now arrived at that Epistle which is beyond question the greatest work of St. Paul. Indeed it has sometimes been regarded as more of a treatise than an Epistle. In very early times it seems to have been circulated in an abridged form, with the merely epistolary portion (chaps. xv., xvi.) omitted. Still there is no denying it, even if it were thus reduced, the title of an Epistle. Every now and then, in the very midst of its argument, the epistolary address occurs; and it is manifest that the Apostle never at any time dropped from his thoughts the fact that he was writing a letter to the members of a Church.

St. Paul had finished the journey in which we found him engaged at our last notice, and had settled down at Corinth for the winter. At some time during this stay he probably wrote the Epistle to the Galatians, as we have already shown. The great subject which the fickleness of the Galatian Church had brought into prominence, had been much before his mind. 'Ye are all children of God through faith in Christ Jesus;' this wrought, and was kept fermenting by the Divine Spirit in his thoughts, and, as centuries after in him who was to enforce the great doctrine in ages of corruption, so now in the ear of the Apostle of the Gentiles, 'The just shall live by faith,' was ever sounding. Coincident with this engrossing of his thoughts by this one great theme, came news from the now growing and important Church in the metropolis of the world; news that in it, as so often elsewhere, the Jew and Gentile elements were not in Christian accord; that questions of precedence and questions of observance wanted settling among them. What more natural, than that the Apostle should regard the tidings thus brought as furnishing an opportunity for laying forth the great doctrine of 'Life by Faith' for the Church of God? He had long been intending to visit the Roman Church. It had been founded by no Apostle, but apparently owing to the concurrence of all men from all parts at the capital. This had brought together Christian converts in sufficient numbers to form a considerable church. It is an absolute historical necessity to assume this origin of the Christian body at Rome. For St. Paul declares, Romans xv. 20, that it was not his practice to build where other Apostles had laid the foundation; and further to clench this as applicable to Rome, he formally takes charge of them as the Apostle of the Gentiles, and speaks of his hitherto prevented visit as intended to bestow on them some formal gift of apostolic grace (chap. i. 4). We may notice in passing, that all trace is wanting in historical fact of St. Peter having founded the Church of Rome. That he had *not been there before* St. Paul's Epistle, is certain; that he could not *found* the Church *after* St. Paul had written, is certain; that he did not live and exercise authority after St. Paul, is certain from primitive tradition, which makes him suffer martyrdom at Rome together with St. Paul. His twenty-five years' popedom is the veriest and silliest fable; would have been, even did history leave place for it, a dereliction of his special office as Apostle of the circumcision, and an invasion of the province of another. And this popedom of St. Peter, together with the notion of his having founded the Roman Church, is repudiated by many of the ablest among the Romanists themselves.

This Church then thus founded, what was it? It was of necessity the most important Christian community in the world. It would be sure to receive the greatest future accessions; it had the advantage of the greatest publicity, and the widest ventilation, for any truth delivered to it.

An occasion then having arisen for a letter to explain and settle the misconceptions which had grown up among the Romans, what wonder if the great Apostle availed himself of it to lay forth to them the whole dispensation of God's grace to Jew and Gentile? What wonder if he determined to expand the thoughts of the Epistle to the Galatians, to put into full logical order and extension the matters there boldly and roughly declared, to make a fair and more voluminous copy of the 'big writing' which his own hand had traced in the fervour of his heart to the rapidly apostatizing Church? Opportunities were doubtless frequent for transmitting a letter from any part of the Roman world to the great metropolis. But at the present moment an unusually favourable one occurred. Phœbe, a deaconess of the Church at Kenchrea, the port of Corinth, was travelling to Rome. She had won, by her acts of beneficence to the Church and to himself, the Apostle's approval and esteem. She therefore (for we can hardly otherwise understand chap. xvi. 1, 2) becomes the bearer of the Epistle.

An interesting consideration remains for us before we enter upon the contents of the letter, respecting a point of some apparent difficulty. The letter was most probably sent from Corinth in the spring of A.D. 58. Three years after, in the beginning of A.D. 61, the Apostle arrived a prisoner at Rome. The Jews resorted to him, and he addressed them, as we read in Acts xxviii. There we find the Jews having very scant knowledge about St. Paul himself, and hardly any about the Christian sect. They wished to know more about him and it. Now some have asked how this could have been, if, three years before, the faith of the Roman Christians was spoken of throughout all the world (Rom. i. 8). The answer seems to me to be very plain. Those who came together to St. Paul's lodging were not Christians, but simply Jews, resident in Rome. Their knowledge of their own (to them) apostate brethren would be necessarily but small, and would be dissimulated by them as being smaller than it really was. They, having heard of Saul of Tarsus and his doings, assemble to inquire of him about himself and the sect which he has joined; and speak to him in a manner most likely to elicit that knowledge. The interview reveals to us nothing about the Christian Church in Rome at the time. Of them we first gain a glimpse, when we learn that during the seven days' stay of the Apostle at Puteoli, they heard of it, and sent a deputation many miles out of Rome to meet him (Acts xxviii. 15). And another, when we are told that 'Paul received all that came in unto him, preaching the kingdom of God, and teaching those things which concern the Lord Jesus Christ.' (Acts xxviii. 30, 31.)

And now let us come to the Epistle itself. It is very important that the English reader should have the contents and argument of it clearly set out before him. For it is one of those treatises which can hardly be understood, except by seeing it as a whole, and marking the progress of the argument from one step to another.

The first chapter opens with the apostolic greeting, conceived, however, in terms more solemn and stately than ordinary. It would seem as if the Apostle had before his mind the metropolitan majesty of the imperial city of Rome, and set against it the majesty of the great revelation of the Son of God, the fulfilment of the world-long promise, the temple of the indwelling Spirit poured out upon mankind, the firstborn from the dead. He looked upon all the world obedient to the sway of Rome, and he thought upon that wider and grander obedience of faith which should bring under its sway all nations of the earth. (There is not a grander thing in literature than this) opening of the Epistle to the Romans. After this he speaks of his desire to see them, and so is led to his readiness to proclaim the glad tidings at Rome also. Yes, even at Rome, in all its power and splendour; for he felt no shame in doing this, no shrinking at standing forth, a solitary man, in the pomp of the Forum, in the crowd of the Suburra, before plebs and patricians, before flamens and augurs, before prefects and Cæsars, and announcing that which is the power of God unto salvation to every one that believeth; first to God's chosen people—they were committed specially to others; then to the Gentile nations, among which this was first. Thus he arrives at the enunciation of his great theme. This Gospel is the power of God to every one that believeth, because in it God's righteousness is unveiled to the eye of faith; and the more, the higher degrees of faith are attained. And this was no new idea, no invention of his; but it had been long ago declared by the word of the prophets that the way to life was to become righteous by believing God.

From this point (chap. i. 18) begins the doctrinal exposition of the mighty truth just declared, that the Gospel is the power of God unto salvation to every one that believeth, by uncovering to man the righteousness of God. And first, man must be made to see that he has no righteousness of his own. First, then, comes a revelation of wrath against men for keeping down or holding back the truth of God in unrighteousness. And first for the majority of mankind—the Gentile world.

Then follows that terrible description in plain words of the fearful state of the heathen world, so abundantly confirmed by the classic writers, so testified by the Epigrams of Martial and the walls of Pompeii. And here let me boldly say that I thank God for such passages as this in our Bibles. I thank God for some of those chapters in the Old Testament from which pretended modern delicacy shrinks in an age which has no other opportunity of hearing sin called by its true name, and put into connexion with declarations of God's wrath. May the day never come when the mistaken fancy that such words should not be publicly read in our churches will cause their exclusion from our table of lessons, as some have threatened.

The Apostle goes on to show that in this matter of sinfulness before God, all are alike: that none has a right to set himself up above and judge another; for that man's unworthiness and God's long-suffering are universal. And so he passes gradually to the case of the Jews, whom by-and-by (chap. ii. 17) he directly addresses, especially with reference to their supposed, and real, advantages over others in the knowledge of God: contrasting the pride of the Jews in their law and their God, with their actual disobedience to both; showing that by the works of the law shall no flesh be justified: and that Abraham's real advantage was his faith, by which he was justified before God without the works of the law. And this justification by faith was not his alone, but shall be ours also, if we believe the resurrection of Jesus from the dead. This is the state of the main line of argument as far as the end of chap. iv. With chap. v. begins the general statement, for Jew and Gentile alike, of the blessed consequences of this justification by faith; of the nature and extent of the blessings bestowed on us by the death and resurrection of Christ; their extent being as wide in their saving influence as Adam's sin was in ruining: yea, wider, because the nature of a free gift is of itself wider and more spreading than that of a prescribed and limited condemnation. And the very use of the law was this, to make abundant and multiply the grace of God, by creating sin, over which grace might triumph. And now with chap. vi. the Apostle begins one of those wonderful courses of what we may call retrogressive argument, with which this Epistle abounds. If it be true that the more sin, the more grace, then we have only to continue in sin that grace may the more abound. This he puts as a question, Is it to be so? Is it after all to come to this, that the Gospel, which was to do away with sin, encourages sin? Let it not be: God forbid. The very essence and condition of the covenant of grace is, deadness to sin, and of this the rite which admitted us into Christ was symbolical. And now comes in, as ever in the Apostle's arguments, a fresh element, introduced by the reply to the objection—the new life of righteousness springing up coincidentally with the death to sin, and owing to the same influence of union with Christ. Not only are we one with Him in His death, but one with Him also in His resurrection; if we died with Him, we also live with Him. And, therefore, we have no life unto sin for sin, and are bound to slay it in our bodies and live for God. This we can do, for sin shall not conquer us, we not being under the law, which is its great instrument, but under grace. Not that (and here again comes in the objection in an interrogative form) we may therefore commit acts of sin, because we have no fear of being brought under its dominion: for then we should be actually putting ourselves under its dominion, from which we have been freed. Besides, its fruit—we ourselves being judges of it in our former lives—is shame, and ends in death, its wages: whereas we are servants of God, being made holy, and being heirs of His gift, everlasting life.

But now this assertion, that we are not under the law, but under grace, comes in for further explanation and elucidation. In ch. vii. 1—4, he illustrates it by the comparison of a woman freed from the marriage vow by the death of her husband. Then he carries the subject on, by showing that, as the law was the multiplier of sin, tempting the evil in our hearts to break forth into transgression, so we, when we were under it, served in the bondage of the letter, and brought forth fruit unto death; but now, having died with Christ, we are freed from the law, and serve in the newness of the spirit, in liberty, which is where the Spirit of God is.

But then does it follow that the law was sin? It looks very like it, if it brought out and multiplied sin. But it may not be. It is not sin, but the detector of sin. Sin is brought out by it, and its working discerned. It is not the poison, but the test. And here the Apostle introduces a very remarkable form of illustration, suddenly turning his discourse into the first person, and relating apparently his own experience. The inquiry into and explanation of this are so important, and the progress of the argument from this point to the end of ch. viii. so unbroken, that we must here make that pause which the length and weight of the Epistle necessitate, and reserve the rest of it for our next part.

We will here give our usual corrections of the text, and the English rendering, for the former portion of the Epistle.

As regards the text, the following alterations should be made, in order to conform it to the testimony of the most eminent and trustworthy authorities. It will be observed that they are very few in comparison to the number in some other books of the New Testament.

In chap. i. 16, omit the words "*of Christ.*" In ver. 29, omit '*fornication.*' In ver. 31, omit '*implacable.*'

In ch. ii. 17, for '*Behold,*' substitute 'But if,' which is the reading of all our earliest MSS. In the Greek the two expressions differ by one letter only, and that letter one frequently expressed or not, indifferently, in the ancient manner of writing.

In ch. iii. 22, 'and upon all,' is omitted by most of our early MSS. This may have been done by a transcriber's mistake: as nothing is more common than to find that the copyist's eye passed from a word or a syllable to the same word or syllable again occurring near. But this omission requires notice, being found in so many ancient MSS. of different origin. In ver. 28, our earliest MSS. are divided between 'therefore,' and 'for:' see below in corrections of rendering.

In ch. iv. 1, for '*father*,' read 'forefather.' In ver. 19, many of our oldest authorities omit the word 'not.' If we adopt this reading, the meaning will be, 'He considered, was well aware of, his own body, &c., and, &c.; but staggered not,' &c.

In ch. v. 1, occurs a very remarkable various reading. Where our text has '*we have* peace,' all the very ancient MSS., without exception, have 'let us have peace.' The difference in the Greek is only that of one letter: echŏmen, with the short o, or omicron (o), being 'we have,' and echōmen, with the long o, or omega (ω), being 'let us have.'

What complicates the difficulty of deciding between the two in this case is, that the two letters are not unfrequently interchanged in the early MSS., where no difference of meaning could have been intended. Thus the Vatican MS. reads, 'As let us have opportunity,' in Gal. vi. 10, which would be nonsense, and cannot have been meant; the Alexandrine and Parisian read, 'let us which have believed enter into rest,' in Heb. iv. 3, of which the same may be said; and the Alexandrine reads, 'let us receive,' of which the same may be said, in 1 John iii. 22. So we are really uncertain whether this is to be treated as a substantial variation or not. If we adopt 'let us have,' the meaning will be, although unexpected and somewhat obscure, yet in substance the same, 'let us have,' *i.e.*, having it, let us recognise that possession, and act accordingly. In ver. 2, omit '*by faith.*' In ver. 6, for 'for when,' the Vatican MS. has, 'if, that is, when.' In ver. 8, the same MS., for 'God,' has 'He.' Many of the MSS. which read 'God,' have it variously placed in the sentence: a sure sign that it is a later addition.

In ch. vi. 1, for '*shall we* continue,' almost all our early MSS. have, 'are we to continue,' *i.e.*, 'may we continue.' The received text has hardly any MS. authority. In ver. 11, omit '*our Lord:*' and in ver. 12, omit '*it in.*'

In ch. vii. 6, for '*that being dead* wherein we were held,' all our earliest MSS. have, 'having died unto that wherein we were held.'

The necessary changes in rendering, owing to the mistakes of our translators, are far more numerous. Indeed, it is hardly possible for the merely English reader to make himself master of this argument of this great Epistle, so much has it been obscured for want of accurate translation.

In ch. i. 5, for 'obedience *to the* faith,' substitute 'obedience of faith.' In ver. 8, '*published*,' should be 'spoken of.' In ver. 10, for '*I might have a prosperous journey*,' 'I shall have a way opened.' In ver. 12, for 'by *the mutual faith both of you and me*,' 'each by the faith that is in the other, both yours and mine.' In ver. 17, the words 'the just,' or 'the righteous shall live by faith,' might also be understood, 'the righteous by faith,' 'those that are righteous by faith,' 'shall live.' In ver. 18, '*hold*,' ought to be 'hold back,' or 'hold down,' *i.e.*, having it and knowing it, quench its testimony and its power by their unrighteous lives. In ver.

19, 'that which *may be* known,' ought to be, 'that which is known.' The Apostle is speaking, not of what they might have known of God, but of what, as matter of fact, they did know. In ver. 21, '*imaginations*,' ought to be 'reasonings.' In ver. 29, '*haters of God*,' should be 'hated of (or, by) God;' for such is the meaning of the word. It was an epithet used by the ancient writers to signify any one given up to crimes which were abhorrent from our idea of the divine equity and mercy. In ver. 32, '*knowing*,' is not strong enough for the word in the original, which signifies 'knowing well,' being perfectly acquainted with.

In ch. ii. 5, for '*against* the day,' substitute 'in the day.' In ver. 8, for 'them that *are contentious*,' 'them that seek their own.' In ver. 22, for '*commit sacrilege*,' substitute 'rob temples.' In ver. 26, '*righteousness*' should be 'ordinances.' In ver. 27, 'through the letter' is better than '*by* the letter.' It is the *medium* through which, not the instrument by which, that is spoken of.

In ch. iii. ver. 3 should stand thus:—'For what if some were unfaithful? shall their unfaithfulness make void the faithfulness of God?' In ver. 5, '*taketh vengeance*' should be 'inflicteth his wrath.' It may be well to remark once for all on the expression, 'God forbid' (ver. 6). It is not the literal rendering of the original, which is, 'Let it not happen!' but it comes the nearest to its meaning in solemnity and earnestness of denial and deprecation. In ver. 8, the meaning would be clearer if the ellipsis of the original were somewhat more filled up: 'And why should we not say, as we be,' &c. In the end of this verse, '*damnation*' does not mean what we now commonly understand by it, and would be better therefore expressed by 'condemnation.' In ver. 19, 'become guilty before' should be 'be brought under the judgment of.' In ver. 20, '*therefore*' should be 'because.' In ver. 21, '*without*' should be 'apart from.' In ver. 23, the verb '*come*' is ambiguous in tense. It is very commonly joined with the auxiliary 'have'—'All have sinned, and have come short.' But this is wrong, for the verb is *present*. It should therefore be expressed by some word which may indicate this—as, 'All have sinned, and fall short of the glory of God.' In ver. 25, '*in* His blood' should be 'by His blood.' As it stands, it is open to the mistake of supposing that the words 'faith in His blood' are to be connected, which is not the case, and, if it were, would give us an unexampled form of expression. In ver. 28, 'for' is better than 'therefore' (see the former set of corrections), seeing that this is not an inference concluding an argument, but a reason stated in justification of the expression just used, 'the law of faith ;' and for '*conclude,*' which is not the sense of the verb, but has been given to it to support the idea that this is the *conclusion* of an argument, substitute 'reckon ;' and for '*without,*' 'apart from.'

Ch. iv. ver. 1, ought to stand, 'What then shall we say that Abraham our forefather hath found as pertaining to the flesh?' For no distinction is here made, as in ch. ix. 3, 5, between his fleshly and his spiritual paternity; but fleshly gain and privilege are contrasted with those which are spiritual, in the case of the same, our forefather Abraham.

In ch. v. 2, render, 'through whom we have also had our access, &c.; and we glory in the hope of the glory of God.' In ver. 3, 4, for '*patience,*' 'endurance ;' and for '*experience,*' 'approval,' both *twice.* In ver. 5, for '*the love of God,*' 'God's love.' It is not our love to God, but His to us, which is spoken of. In the same verse, for '*is given,*' 'was given.' In ver. 11, for '*the atonement,*' 'our reconciliation.' In ver. 12, for '*passed upon,*' 'spread through unto;' and for '*have sinned,*' 'sinned.' In ver. 15, for '*offence,*' 'trespass;' and for '*free gift,*' 'gift of grace;' also, for '*many*' (twice), 'the many,' *i.e.*, all men. This mis-translation is a grievous instance of the way in which our translators allowed their own theological opinions to bias their rendering of Scripture. In the Latin, and those versions that were made from it, the mistake was obvious, as the Latin language has no definite article; but King James's translators professed diligently to compare with the original Greek, and ought to have known better. In the same verse, for '*the grace of God and the gift by grace, which is by one man, Jesus Christ, hath abounded unto many,*' 'did the grace of God and his free gift abound unto the many by the grace of the one man Jesus Christ.' In ver. 16, for '*offences,*' 'trespasses.' This distinction, here and before, is important. The Apostle is speaking of the state of things under the law, when sin was not only an offence, but a *trespass* of a rule laid down. In ver. 17, for '*free* gift,' 'gift;' and for '*one,*' 'the one.

Ver. 18 should stand, 'Therefore as through one trespass the issue was unto all men to condemnation: even so through one righteous act the issue was unto all men to justification of life.' In ver. 19, for '*one man's* disobedience,' 'the disobedience of the one man;' and again twice, for '*many*,' 'the many:' see in ver. 15: and for '*one*,' 'the one.' In ver. 20, 'then the law came in besides, that the trespass might be multiplied. But when sin was multiplied, grace did beyond measure abound.' In ver. 21, for '*sin hath reigned unto death*,' 'sin reigned in death.'

In ch. vi. ver. 2, for '*are dead*,' substitute 'died,' the time spoken of being that of our baptism, as in the next verse. In ver. 4, for '*are* buried,' 'were buried;' and for '*by baptism into death*,' 'through our baptism into his death:' and for '*by* the glory,' 'through the glory.' In ver. 5, read 'if we have become united to the likeness of his death, surely we shall be also to the likeness of his resurrection.' In ver. 6, for '*is* crucified,' 'was crucified.' In ver. 7, the word rendered 'set free,' is, literally, 'justified.' In ver. 8, for '*be dead*,' 'died.' Ver. 10 would be better and more literally, 'For the death that he died, he died unto sin once; but the life that he liveth, he liveth unto God.' In ver. 13, for '*are alive from the dead,*' 'were dead and are alive.' In ver. 17, read 'ye obeyed from the heart the form of doctrine whereunto ye were delivered.' In ver. 19, for '*have* yielded,' 'yielded;' and also in ver. 22, for '*holiness,*' 'sanctification.' In ver. 21, '*then*' is ambiguous; it may be the 'then' of *inference,* or the 'then' of *time.* It *is* the latter. Render therefore, 'at that time,' and the ambiguity is escaped. Also, after 'at that time,' put a note of interrogation, and proceed, 'Things whereof,' &c. In ver. 23, for '*through,*' 'in.'

In ch. vii. 1, for '*speak to men,*' substitute 'am speaking to men.' As the verse now stands, it looks as if the Apostle suddenly addressed himself to a new class of readers; whereas he means that those whom he is throughout addressing are men that feared the law. In ver. 3, for '*be dead,*' 'die.' In ver. 4, for '*are become,*' 'were made;' and for '*married,*' 'joined.' In ver. 5, for '*did work* . . . . *to bring,*' 'were active . . . . so as to bring.' In ver. 6, for '*in newness of spirit,*' 'in the newness of the spirit.'

VIII.

THE EPISTLE TO THE ROMANS.

(*Second Part.*)

WE resume our summary of the contents of this great Epistle at that point (ver. 7) in ch. vii. where the Apostle suddenly assumes the first person, carrying it on as far as ch. viii. 2, where it is again dropped. And in order to master the meaning of this section of the argument, we must be able clearly to set before ourselves who it is that here speaks. Is it the Apostle in his own person, or is it the Apostle in the person of some one else? And let not the latter seem to any improbable. Nothing is more common (the present writer is conscious of the practice in his own sermons) than to introduce in the first person a general example of that which one is adducing or arguing for, without any intention of identifying that which is said with any portion of one's own experience. Still, the practice has its rules and limits. It usually applies to the present and the future of the person thus designated, but can hardly be extended to the past. One might say, for example, after describing the sympathy of our blessed Lord, 'Well then, I see but One who can feel for all my infirmities. I have no scruples, no backwardness in coming to such a Friend, such a Brother, and pouring out all my heart to Him.' While we speak thus, we are well understood to be using general language, and referring, not to our own, but to human experience in general. But if I were to say, in the past tense, 'Well, I felt all this: I took into account that He who was perfect God, was also perfect Man: I came without scruple or timidity, and I poured out my heart before Him,'—who would not naturally suppose that I was describing something that had happened to myself? Could such language be used, and yet the meaning have no such reference? Would not one who thus spoke, intending only to give a general example, be fairly chargeable with clumsiness and mal-adroitness? And are these at all the faults of the writer with whom we are now dealing?

Granted, that St. Paul's arguments are not conducted according to the set procedure of a logical treatise: that his fervid spirit is continually carrying him out of bounds, and causing him to digress into the by-paths of the road along which he is conducting his reader; granted, that he rather bounds over the fences of dialectic rule, than walks between them: yet in the midst of all his fervour and irregularity, there is ever the most delicate tact, the most rapidly responsive sense of possibility of being misunderstood or misapplied: nothing like awkwardness, nothing like mal-adroitness. We cannot suppose him to have spoken in the first person, and in the past tense, without really meaning to relate things which have happened to himself. If he is writing here in the person of all mankind, or in that of the Jewish people, all we can say is, that he has forgotten his usual clearness and elegance, and is writing clumsily and unintelligibly. If we shrink from bringing these charges against him, we are, it seems to me, bound to adopt the other alternative, and to believe that he is describing his own past life, at some time or other of its history. But now comes the question, at *what* time? And here opinions have been various. We may best perhaps discuss them as we pass on in the exposition of the passage.

He has spoken before (ver. 7) of our having died to the law, and of the stirrings of sin, which were, *i.e.* took place, by means of the law. And by this strong language, some risk has been incurred that his reader may imagine the law itself to be identical with sin; seeing that we are dead also to sin—seeing that sin works within us, and by means of sin we are stirred and moved to sin. This error he now proceeds to combat; and he does it, not by any general assertion of what takes place in the human heart in general, but by what he was conscious of in his own history. Had he spoken generally, the influence might not have been sure: a reader might have stopped short of a living conviction that it was all true of individual men; but now that he gives an actual experience of his own, he states what none can deny, and what finds an echo in the history of a thousand souls. 'The law is NOT SIN; far be the thought. Yet (not '*nay*,' which obscures and blunders the whole) so near is the law to being sin, that the law first introduced me to sin—first made me acquainted with it. But how? I was in the habit of coveting. I did it, unconscious of any fault. But the law *came* in, became heeded by me, with its voice, 'Thou shalt not covet:' and my coveting started up into sin, became sinful, to me, and in my esteem. And, as we are ever prone to enjoy that which is forbidden, sin thus got life and zest for me, and I indulged in all manner of coveting, just because stolen waters were sweet, and sin wrought upon my human perverseness. Before this forbidding voice spoke within me, before the commandment 'came,' *I* lived; was alive and well; enjoyed a kind of innocence and freewill of my own; but after this, not I, but sin in me, lived and wrought its will. And the very prohibition which was for life, by waking up the sense of sin, and the desire for sin, killed *me*, set me lusting for that evil which is death, and slew my freewill and my former peace and joy. Yet notice, that it was not the commandment itself, but sin, the sinful principle in me, awakened into life by the commandment, that thus killed me: and the commandment only brought out that which was there before, but latent and dormant: brought it out, for good, and for the behalf and the life, of the better and worthier 'I,' the 'I' in conflict with sin, the complex man, the 'I Paul' of the time present.

And now, and from this point, the narrative of the past ceases, and the description of the present begins. In the Paul then writing to them, these motions toward sin remained; this conviction of sin through the law continued. In the breast of the Apostle, there was an uncertainty and a conflict: what he did he knew not (not, *allowed* not: see in corrections below),—*i.e.*, as Chrysostom admirably explains it, 'he was in the dark, staggered, and struck down, he knew not how.' He did not the good he wished; the evil that he wished not, that he did. And this new conflict is a testimony that it is not I, not the inner man, not the very person in his full personality, that do this sin, but another, even the living principle of sin within me. The real inner man delights in the law of God; but this other in the law of sin. And this produces a state of despair, yea, even of a living death, the consequence of the coming in of the law, holy as it is, and awakening sin within a man. How is Paul, how is any man, to get deliverance from this body of death? Thanks to God through Christ, the issue has been won, the deliverance effected. Condemnation has passed away for them that are in Christ (see corrections below).

The law of the Spirit of life has set them free from the law of sin and death. The law could not do this; it was a carnal commandment, working through the medium of the flesh, and could go no further; but God did it, by sending His Son in the likeness of that flesh of sin, and by making Him a victim for sin. Thus sin stands condemned in the flesh; thus, on the other hand, the demands of the law are fulfilled in us who walk, not after the flesh, but after the spirit; and thus, too, though the flesh is still subject to death by reason of sin, the spirit is heir of life by reason of righteousness, and shall, moreover, by reason of its being dwelt in by God's Spirit, bring up the mortal body also, in virtue of Christ's resurrection, and by the exertion of the same power of the Father.

Well then, what is the inference? This: that we owe nothing to the flesh, so as to induce us to live after it. To do so would be to die spiritually. Life is bound up with sonship in God's family; and they who are His sons are led by His Spirit, who is to them the witness of their adoption. This sonship also brings heirship with it; co-heirship with Him with whom we are now suffering—with whom we shall be hereafter glorified.

Then follows a digression—which, like others in St. Paul, is not really a digression, but ministers admirably to the main argument—on suffering, decay, death, as ordinances in God's creation, ministering to future glory, in which even creation itself shall partake. That we ourselves share in these, is no reason why we should ultimately fail of glory, or be separated from the love of God. This separation, indeed, nothing can effect; God has bestowed on us His own Son as a pledge that He will, with Him, freely give us all things. So that no present nor future evil, no power in heaven or earth, can separate us from the love of God in Jesus Christ our Lord.

And thus the mighty argument is brought to an end. The remainder of the Epistle is spent in the determination of various points of interest as related to the position of Jew and Gentile, in God's dealings, and in the church of the time. Meanwhile, however, the great argument is supplemented by the views of God's wisdom and love, and does not reach its final conclusion till ch. xii., where the Apostle gathers up all in general exhortations, grounded on this review of God's mercies to Jew and Gentile.

From that point, he begins giving directions for Christian conduct under various circumstances; directions grounded, no doubt, in the special composition and position of the Roman Church. Among these are, commands as to obedience to the earthly powers set over them: as to observance or non-observance of times and days, and the abstinence from certain meats: things, St. Paul rules it, absolutely indifferent in themselves, and to be arranged by the rules of charity and respect by one to the scruples of another. Even Christ pleased not himself: neither ought we to have regard only to our own sentiments and desires. Jew with Gentile, Gentile with Jew, ought to glorify God in common: both were contemplated in the mission of Jesus Christ, and spoken of in its prophetic announcements. And the Apostle himself was specially ordered to minister to the Gospel of God, in offering, as it were, as a priest, the Gentiles unto Him as an acceptable sacrifice. This to accomplish had been the object of his apostolic life: and in pursuance of that purpose, he was in due time coming to them, after having carried the contributions of the churches to Jerusalem. Meantime, might God bless them, and might a favourable issue of this his purpose be granted, so that he might come to them in joy by the will of God.

The last chapter is spent in commending to them Phœbe the deaconess, the bearer of this letter, and in salutations of them, and to them from the brethren who were with him. In this concluding chapter there are several points of interest to every age of the Church. First, we have Phœbe, deaconess of the church at Kenchrea, the port of Corinth, commended in such an especial manner to the church at Rome, as to make it more than probable that she was the bearer of the Epistle. We see woman in the early church already in a position of trust and high usefulness: a position, let me observe, which she retains in the Roman Catholic communion to this day, in conjunction with various conditions opposed to Christian freedom and our Lord's commands, but which, owing to those conditions having been justly repudiated by the Reformed Churches, she has very generally lost among ourselves. One of the gravest problems of our own and of the coming age will be, to bring in female help to the work of the Church, and woman into an accredited position in her service, without any admixture of the 'votal' element; without any permanent obligations to poverty, to what is called 'obedience,' to what is mistaken for 'chastity.' Another matter of interest in this chapter is, the examples which it gives us of the refined delicacy and courtesy of the great Apostle. 'To whom not only I give thanks, but all the churches of the Gentiles;' 'which were in Christ before me;' 'Salute Rufus, the elect in the Lord, and his mother—*and mine;*' *i.e.*, his mother, whom I also love as a son.

Yet another point of interest is this. On the southern side of Rome, as you approach the gate now called the Porta San Sebastiano,—not far from the Arch of Drusus, under which St. Paul passed as he entered the city with the brethren,—is a garden, containing the 'columbarium,' or 'pigeon-house,' of the 'family' of Nero. It may be necessary to inform the English reader, that these 'columbaria' are so called from their containing a number of small recesses like pigeon-holes, in which are deposited the ashes of the dead; and that the 'family' of a Roman prince or noble comprehended all who lived in his court, his relatives, freedmen, and slaves. And with thus much explanation, we may repeat the result of our own researches in the columbarium of the family of Nero. Among the names inscribed on the memorial tablets there, we found Tryphæna (ver. 12), Tryphosa (ver. 12), Hermes (ver. 14), Hermas (ver. 14), and Junias (ver. 7).

Another matter of interest in this chapter is the remarkable doxology with which it concludes. It would appear as if at first the Epistle had concluded with ver. 24; and that the Apostle, at some subsequent period, on reading it over, had added the doxology. This idea is confirmed by the state of the readings of the ancient MSS. (see below); and by the fact that the style of this doxology is not that of the rest of the Epistle, but rather that of St. Paul's later writings, the Epistles to Timothy and that to Titus.

Our list of corrections to be made in the text of our present portion (Rom. vii. 7—end) will be of necessity somewhat long: more, however, as regards errors of translation, than varieties of reading.

To the latter class belong the following:—In ch. vii. 18, for '*I find not*,' read 'is not (present).' In ver. 25, for 'I thank God,' read 'Thanks be to God.'

In ch. viii. 1, omit the clause '*who walk not after the flesh, but after the Spirit.*' It has probably been interpolated here from ver. 4. In sense, at first-sight, it fits in well; here, as there, being a distinctive and correct statement of *those in Christ* to whom there is no condemnation; but on looking further, it clearly appears to be out of place here, since at present the assertion is *general*, respecting all those who are in Christ, and afterwards the distinction is raised, and their true and spiritual character defined. In ver. 11, 'by His *Spirit*,' should be 'by reason of, or because of, His Spirit.' In ver. 26, for 'infirmit*ies*,' read 'infirmity,' or 'weakness.' The meaning is not here, that the Spirit helps our infirmit*ies*, generally: but that He helps in this particular point our weakness, our inability to wait with patience for that which we hope for. In the same verse, the words 'for us' are wanting in most of the ancient authorities.

In ch. ix. 19, for '*why*,' read 'why then.' In ver. 31 (end), omit the words 'of righteousness.' In ver. 32, for 'the works of the law,' many of our ancient authorities read simply 'works.' In same verse, omit the word '*for*,' and arrange thus: 'Because pursuing after it not by faith, but as by works, they stumbled against the stone of stumbling.' In ver. 33, for '*whosoever*,' read 'he that.'

In ch. x. 1, the insertion of '*Israel*' is not justified. It should stand, 'and my supplication to God on their behalf is for salvation.' In ver. 17, for '*God*,' read 'Christ.'

In ch. xi. 6, the whole latter portion, 'But if it is of works, it is no more grace ; for otherwise work is no more work,' is omitted in several of our oldest MSS. It is very possible that the omission may have been made by mistake, on account of the similarity of the two sentences of which the verse consists : so that it is best to leave the words in the text, and mark them as doubtful. In ver. 18, for 'the root *and* fatness,' 'the root of the fatness.' In ver. 22, instead of 'toward thee, *goodness*,' read, 'toward thee, God's goodness.' It stands thus in our principal ancient authorities ; and these emphatic repetitions are customary with St. Paul.

In ch. xii. 11, instead of 'serving the Lord,' some of our ancient MSS. have 'serving the time,' *i.e.*, the opportunity : watching for opportunities. The difference in the Greek is very slight, 'Kurio' being 'the Lord,' and 'kairo' 'the time.' It is not quite certain which of the two is original; but internal evidence seems to predominate for 'the Lord,' inasmuch as Christians may be ordered to *watch* oportunities, or the times, but hardly could be ordered to *serve* (be in bondage to) them.

In ch. xiii. 3, for '*good works*,' read 'the good work.' In ver. 7, omit '*therefore*,' In ver. 9, omit '*Thou shalt not bear false witness.*'

In ch. xiv. 4, for '*God*,' read 'the Lord.' In ver. 6, the latter sentence, 'and he that regardeth not the day to the Lord he doth not regard it,' is omitted by all our earliest MSS., although inserted in the most ancient versions. The omission may here also have originated in mistake, the eye of the transcriber passing from the end of the former sentence to the exactly similar end of this one. As ancient testimony is almost unanimous, we are bound to mark the words as of doubtful authenticity, remembering, however, as we do so, that there may have been other reasons than mere accident for their exclusion. They were as likely to appear objectionable to the rigorous observers of days in ancient times, as they are inexplicable to the rigid sabbatarian in our own. In ver. 9, instead of '*both died and rose and revived*,' read 'died and lived;' the latter word, by the context, meaning, lived again after his resurrection. In ver. 10, for '*Christ*,' read 'God.' In ver. 15, for '*But* if,' read 'For if.' In ver. 18, for '*in these things*,' read 'in this,' or 'herein.' In ver. 22, for '*Hast thou faith?* have it,' read 'The faith which thou hast, have it.'

In ch. xv. 7, most of our ancient authorities, instead of '*us*,' have 'you.' In ver. 8, for '*Now* I say,' read 'For I say,' and omit '*Jesus.*' In ver. 11, for '*laud Him all ye people*,' read 'let all the people praise Him.' In ver. 19, 'Spirit of God,' the ancient MSS. vary, some having 'Holy Spirit,' and the Vatican has 'Spirit' only, which latter was probably the original reading. In ver. 24, the words '*I will come to you*' are wanting in all our most ancient authorities. They have evidently been inserted to fill up the sense, which seemed imperfect without them. But this will not be so, if we read the sentence thus, 'But now I have no more place in these parts, and have had these many years a longing to come unto you, whenever I take my journey into Spain.' The English reader must be reminded that there are *no stops* in the ancient MSS., and that the whole punctuation and arrangement of sentences in Scripture is purely a matter of modern guess-work. In ver. 29, omit '*the gospel of.*'

In ch. xvi. 3, for '*Priscilla*' read 'Prisca,' with all our most ancient MSS. (see 2 Tim. iv. 19). In ver. 5, for '*Achaia*' read 'Asia.' In ver. 6, for 'us' read 'you.' In ver. 16, for '*the churches*' read 'all the churches.' In ver. 18, omit '*Jesus.*' In ver. 20, omit '*Amen.*' Ver. 24 is omitted by our four most eminent MSS.; and verses 25—27 are omitted altogether by some ancient MSS.,—omitted *here*, and inserted after ch. xiv. 23, by others,—and by others inserted in both places. The truth seems to have been, that two different editions of the Epistle were current in apostolic times, one with, and one without, the concluding doxology. See above.

The errors and insufficiencies in *translation* of this portion of the Epistle may be thus described:—

In ch. vii. 7, '*nay*' should rather be 'nevertheless;' and '*lust*' should be 'coveting.' In ver. 8, the words 'by the commandment' ought to be joined to 'wrought in me,' not to what has gone before; and, again, '*concupiscence*' should be 'coveting.' Again, '*was* dead' should be 'is dead.' In ver. 9, '*revived*' should be 'came to life.' In ver. 10, 'the commandment' should be 'the very commandment.' In ver. 11, again, the words 'by the commandment' ought to be joined with what follows, not with what precedes. In ver. 13, '*in me*' should be 'to me.' In ver. 15, '*allow* not' ought to be 'know not.' The original word is that always used for 'to know,' and no other meaning here is either required or justified. In ver. 20, for '*sin* that dwelleth,' 'the sin that dwelleth.' In ver. 21, for '*a* law,' 'this law.' In ver. 23, for '*another* law,' 'a different law.' It is not merely another, but a contrarient law.

In ch. viii. 2, for *hath made* me free,' should stand, 'set me free,' viz., when I received it as my law. In ver. 4, '*righteousness*' ought to be 'righteous demand.' In ver. 6, '*to be carnally minded*' should be 'the mind of the flesh:' and '*to be spiriually minded,*' 'the mind of the Spirit.' In ver. 7, for '*is not subject* . . . . *neither indeed can be,*' substitute, 'doth not submit itself . . . . neither indeed can it.' In ver. 8, for '*so then,*' 'and.' In ver. 10, read 'the body indeed is dead.' In ver. 11, for 'shall *also* quicken,' 'shall quicken even.' In ver. 13, for 'ye *shall* die,' 'ye must die.

The original is, 'ye are about to die,' conveying a more certain and inevitable result than the future tense, which is used afterwards. In ver. 15, for 'ye *have not received*,' 'ye did not receive.' 'Again to fear' is ambiguous; it does not explain whether 'fear' is the noun or the verb. Better say, 'leading back unto fear.' Omit '*have*' before received. In ver. 16, for '*with* our spirit,' 'to our spirit.' In ver. 20, for 'the *creature*,' 'the creation:' also in ver. 21, '*willingly*' is ambiguous. It should be 'of its own will.' For '*hath* subjected the same,' 'made it subject.' In ver. 21, 'the *glorious liberty*' altogether evaporates the meaning. It should be 'the liberty of the glory of the children of God:' that liberty which belongs to the state of glorification of God's children. In ver. 23, 'waiting for' does not fully express the meaning. It is 'waiting for the end of,' 'for the full accomplishment of.' In ver. 24, 'we *are* saved' should be 'we were saved.' For '*yet*,' 'also.' In ver. 26, '*likewise*' should be 'in like manner:' which perhaps 'likewise' may have been meant to represent: but it does not now convey that sense. Verses 33, 34 should probably stand thus: 'Who shall lay anything to the charge of God's elect? Shall God, that justifieth? Who is he that condemneth? Is it Christ that died, yea more, that is also risen again, who is also at the right hand of God, who also maketh intercession for us?'

In ch. ix. 1, for 'my conscience also bearing me witness,' substitute 'my conscience bearing me witness of the same.' In ver. 19, for '*hath resisted*,' 'resisteth.' In ver. 22, for '*the* vessels,' 'vessels.' In ver. 28, for 'he *will finish* the work, and *cut* it short,' 'he is finishing the reckoning, and cutting it short;' and further on, for 'a short *work*,' 'a short reckoning.' In ver. 33, for '*on him*,' '*thereon*,' viz., on the stone.

In ch. x. 5, for '*doeth*,' 'hath done;' and for '*by them*,' 'in it.' In verses 15, 16, '*gospel*' ought to be 'glad tidings,' the word being the same throughout. In ver. 17, '*hearing*' (both times) should be 'report:' the word again is the same throughout: 'So then faith cometh of report, and the report is through the word of Christ.' In ver. 21, for '*to* Israel,' 'in regard to Israel.'

In ch. xi. 1, it should be, 'Did God cast away his people?' And in ver. 2, 'did not cast away,' and 'saith in [the history of] Elijah.' In ver. 11,

'Did they stumble?' and for '*fall*,' 'trespass' (so also in ver. 12). In ver. 17, for '*be* broken off,' 'were broken off:' for 'being a wild olive *tree*,' 'being a wild olive;' and for '*partakest*,' 'wast made partaker.' In ver. 18, for '*boast*,' 'boastest against them.' In ver. 25, '*blindness*' is a misrendering. The meaning of the word is not 'blindness,' but 'hardness,' 'callousness.' In ver. 29, for '*are without repentance*,' 'cannot be repented of.' In ver. 30, for '*have not believed*,' 'were disobedient to;' and for '*unbelief*' below, 'disobedience.' So, also, in verses 31, 32, '*not believed*' should be 'been disobedient,' and '*in unbelief*' should be 'in disobedience.'

In ch. xii. 3, the Apostle plays upon words, as is his manner; and such similarity of sounds ought to be preserved in the English, when it can be done. Here the words might stand, 'not to be high-minded above that which he ought to be, but to be minded so as to be sober-minded.' In ver. 8, '*liberality*' should be 'simplicity.' In ver. 11, '*business*' should be 'diligence' or 'zeal.' It does not refer to the business of this life, but to Christian duties as such. In ver. 16, 'condescending to men of low estate' might also mean 'inclining unto the things that be lowly.' In ver. 20, '*therefore*' should be 'nay, rather.'

In ch. xiii. 1, 2, 3, 'power' should be 'authority.' In ver. 1, 'the *higher powers*' should be 'the authorities that are above him.' For '*are ordained*,' 'have been ordained.' In ver. 2, for '*damnation*,' 'condemnation;' punishment for that disobedience, not eternal perdition, being meant. In ver. 11, it would be better for clearness to insert the word 'first' before 'believed.' In ver. 14, '*make not provision for*' should be 'take no forethought for.'

In ch. xiv. 14, '*by* the Lord Jesus' should be 'in the Lord Jesus.' In ver. 23, for '*damned*,' 'condemned.' In hardly any place where this terrible word is used is its use justified, or is the meaning to be referred to a future life. Our translators have been most inconsistent and capricious in their renderings of this and like words: which is the less excusable, considering what a serious matter was at stake.

In ch. xv. 4, the words should stand, 'that through the patience and the comfort of the Scriptures we might have hope.' The verse is sometimes read as if 'patience' were one thing by itself, and 'comfort of the Scriptures' another by itself. But the two go together:—it is 'patience of the Scriptures, and comfort of the Scriptures': *i.e.*, patience and comfort, both arising from the Scriptures,—produced by their study. In ver. 8, for '*was*,' 'hath been made.' In ver. 9, for '*might glorify*,' 'glorified.' In ver. 12 (end), for '*trust*,' 'hope.' In ver. 16, '*ministering the Gospel*' should be, 'ministering as a priest in the Gospel.' In ver. 20, '*so have I strived to preach*' would be more clearly expressed, 'on this wise making it my ambition to preach.' In ver. 22, for 'I have been much hindered,' 'these many times I have been hindered.' In ver. 26, for '*the poor saints*,' 'the poor among the saints.' In ver. 31, for '*do not believe*,' 'are disobedient.'

In ch. xvi. 1, for '*a servant*,' 'a deaconess.' It seems clear that the word here in the original was used in its official sense in the primitive times of the Church. As it may not be amiss that the English reader should know the proper pronunciation of the names in this chapter, I set them down as we proceed. Ver. 5 : Epænĕtus. Ver. 7 : Andronīcus. The person here called Junia, is most probably Junias, and a man, not a woman.

Ver. 9: The person mentioned as Urbane is not a woman, nor is the word a trisyllable, but the e is mute, and Urb*ane* is Urban, *i.e.*, Urbanus. Ver. 10: Aristobŭlus.* Ver. 14: Asyncrĭtus. Ver. 15: Philólŏgus. In ver. 17, for 'ye have learned,' 'ye learned.' Ver. 21: Sosípăter. In ver. 23, for '*a* brother,' 'our brother.' In ver. 25, for '*since the world began*,' 'during eternal ages.' Ver. 27 should stand, 'to the only wise God rough Jesus Christ, to whom be the glory for ever. Amen.'

* On ver. 11, it is interesting to observe that an epitaph exists, inscribed by Tiberius Claudius Narcissus, a freedman, 'to his affectionate and frugal wife,' Claudia DICAEOSYNA. This was probably one of the 'household of Narcissus' here mentioned, who had taken the name of his patron. The name of the wife is remarkable, as being the Greek word for RIGHTEOUSNESS, so familiar to the readers of St. Paul. Possibly she had an objectionable heathen name, which was changed at her baptism: and the particular word may have been chosen in consequence of this very Epistle.

I am indebted for this information to my friend Professor Plumptre

IX.

THE EPISTLE TO THE COLOSSIANS.

DURING St. Paul's long stay at Ephesus, related in Acts xix., we are told that 'all they that dwelt in Asia heard the word of the Lord Jesus, both Jews and Greeks.' Even remembering that 'Asia' is here used as signifying, of course not the great continent now known by that name, nor even the lesser 'Asia Minor,' but only the Roman province thus designated,—these words must evidently be taken as a vague expression, implying that very many places besides Ephesus were, by means of persons who carried the good tidings thence, made acquainted with the word of the Lord Jesus. And this prepares us for what we read in ch. ii. of the Epistle to the Colossians, that the inhabitants of Colossæ and Laodicea had never seen the Apostle's face in the flesh. He had become the founder of these churches without having visited the cities themselves. To both of these he wrote Epistles. We hear of the Epistle to the Laodiceans in Col. iv. 16, and there only; for it has not come down to us, having been lost. Some silly people are very much shocked at the idea of an inspired apostolic letter having been lost to the Church, and therefore try to quibble away the words of Col. iv. 16, and to understand by the Epistle from Laodicea that written to Philemon, or some other of those which we possess. But these people seem never to have reflected, that in all probability St. Paul wrote multitudes of epistles besides those which have come down to us. Do they think that the Epistle to Philemon is the only private letter which the Apostle ever wrote? or that he did not write all he did write with the same apostolic authority? Do they imagine that his spoken words were less precious than his written ones? and yet the greater part of those has perished.

But the letter to the Colossians has been preserved. To it let us now give our attention.

Colossæ, or Colassæ, as it is written in our earliest manuscripts, was a city on the famous river Mæander, and on the high road from Ephesus to the East. Epaphras, one of its inhabitants, appears to have fallen in with St. Paul at Ephesus, there to have been converted by him, and thence to have returned as a missionary to his native city. With him afterwards were joined, also having been converted by the Apostle at Ephesus, Philemon, his wife Apphia, and (probably) his son Archippus. Their house served for the assembling place (or one of the assembling places) of the church: and they themselves were employed in the sacred ministry.

Of what numbers the church at Colossæ consisted, we are not told. The town itself was one of considerable importance: but had during the reign of Tiberius been desolated by an earthquake, and had never recovered its former prosperity. So that perhaps the number of believers was but small. Still, the prospect of the introduction of error into any portion of the church was reason enough why the Apostle should pour forth his vehement and affectionate spirit in counteracting it. And error of a very serious kind by degrees made its way into the little community at Colossæ. The neighbourhood, and indeed the inhabitants of the whole territory of Phrygia, in which it was situated, were prone to mysticism and fanatical superstitions. Phrygia was the seat of one of the principal forms of mystic heathen worship, that of the goddess Cybele: and ritual observance and ascetic practices seem to have found an especial welcome in the Phrygian atmosphere. The heresy afterwards known as Gnosticism, the teachers of which professed a higher *gnosis*, or knowledge, than others, was beginning to spread in various parts of the Eastern Church. We find it at Colossæ in strange commixture with a leaning to Jewish observances. With these, and the superstitions with which they had become corrupted, the Colossian Gnostics also combined a vainly curious search into the degrees and orders of angelic beings, and a worship of the great hierarchs of the heavenly kingdom. Such a tendency survives even now in the modern superstitions of the Greek Church in the neighbourhood. A great inundation, it is said, once threatened Colossæ, and was dispersed by the descent of the archangel Michael, who opened a chasm into which the waters flowed. (See Conyb. and Howson, 'Life of St. Paul,' ii. p. 411.) Angel-worship was condemned in a council held at the neighbouring Laodicea in the fourth century.

This curious mixture of opinions in the Colossian Church is accounted for partly by the fact told us by Josephus the Jewish historian,—that Alexander the Great sent, in consequence of the disaffection of Lydia and Phrygia, 2,000 Mesopotamian and Babylonian Jews to garrison the towns.

To such a church St. Paul wrote his Epistle: but whence? and when?

Between six and seven years had elapsed since its founding by Epaphras. During this time the Apostle had passed through all that eventful period of his life related in the last nine chapters of the Acts of the Apostles: had escaped the tumult at Ephesus; had crossed into Greece, and wintered at Corinth; had gone up to Jerusalem with forebodings which caused him to take a solemn farewell of the elders of Ephesus at Miletus; had narrowly escaped with his life from his enemies in the Holy City; had lain two years in prison at Cæsarea; had accomplished that long and perilous voyage to Rome. There he was now a prisoner, dwelling with the soldier that kept him in his own hired house, receiving all that came to him without let or hindrance, and labouring for the Gospel of Christ by his tongue and by his pen.

At this time Epaphras comes to Rome and brings him a report from Colossæ. He spoke of their Christian faith, and love, and hope; but he also spoke of much which pained the Apostle's tender heart, and roused his jealousy for the pure faith of Christ. Some time appears to have elapsed after the receipt of this report before St. Paul wrote the epistle. This seems implied in the expression, 'Since the day we heard it, we do not cease to pray for you,' in ch. i. 9. Probably he waited till near the time when Tychicus, whom he sent with the letter, was ready to depart.

Having thus in some measure cleared the ground of preliminary matter, we may proceed to the consideration of the epistle itself.

St. Paul begins with the usual apostolic salutation, associating with himself Timothy, as he had done Silvanus and Timothy in his Epistle to the Thessalonians, Sosthenes in his first Epistle to the Corinthians, and Timothy in his second. The object of the Apostle in this has never been quite understood. Possibly it may have been with a view to carry out the general principle, that in the mouth of two or three witnesses every word should be established; and then, within the limits of this, there may have been special motives, at present unknown to us, for the selection of the particular associates on each occasion. They seldom appear or are thought of again after the first mention; and even where St. Paul uses the plural number, 'we,' he is usually speaking not of himself and his associates, but of himself only.

Having thus opened his Epistle, he proceeds, also after his usual manner, to congratulate the Colossians on the report, which Epaphras had brought, of their faith, and love, and hope. With his thanksgiving for this, he gradually and delicately interweaves his prayer for their further advance in knowledge and practice; and then almost imperceptibly approaches the great subject of their error and his anxiety. Admirable indeed is the way in which, through the long sentence extending from ch. i. 9 to ch. i. 20, the figure of our glorified Lord is made slowly to rise upon the mind's eye in all its love and majesty; care being taken meantime that every separate clause should do its own work in affirming His truth and impugning their error. St. Paul uses the very terms which they had adopted for their vain imaginations: as in the case of the word rendered 'fulness' in ch. i. 19, which is the 'pleroma' of the Gnostic heretics; he overthrows by anticipation their practice of angel-worship by maintaining the absolute and exclusive pre-eminence of Christ over all created beings, and that through the blood of His cross. His blood has made peace; and in that peace they who were once God's enemies are included, provided they continue grounded in the faith, and are not moved away from it. To this end he, the Apostle, is labouring, carrying on, in his work for Christ, the afflictions of Christ to their completion, according to the stewardship of the mystery entrusted to him, which was Christ among them, the hope of the glory to come.

Now, with chap. ii., he approaches nearer to the point concerning which he is at issue with them. His object is, that they who had not seen his face in the flesh (which circumstance seems to increase his responsibility and anxiety) might attain to the thorough knowledge of the mystery of God (see corrections at end). And now appears, what must have been for some time in the mind of an intelligent reader, the motive for his writing this. It is because some one (it would appear from the form of this sentence, as if it had been an individual false teacher) had been endeavouring to lead them captive through his philosophy and vain deceit, according to the traditions of men, according to the rudiments of the world, and not according to Christ. And then their completeness in Him is again insisted on: its past assurances to them in their baptism, which superseded the necessity of that Jewish ordinance into which they were again retreating back, by burying them and raising them again with Him in that living union which it symbolized. And thus, when He suffered on His cross, He blotted out, by fulfilling, all ordinances which were enacted against us; God thus, as it were, divesting Himself of that ministration of angels by which the law was brought in, exalting His Son above them, and in His Person triumphing over them (see corrections of rendering in ch. ii. 15). What then was the result? Why, this. They were to assert their Christian liberty, as being thus complete in Christ. They were to let no man domineer over them and prescribe to them as to the keeping of days, whether feasts, or new-moons, or sabbaths: all these belonged to the old law; between one part of it and another there was no distinction : all these, sabbaths as well as new-moons and feast days, were but shadows of things then to come, which things were now come : the body which cast this shadow before it, being Christ. To the same false teacher belonged the scheme for defrauding them of their Christian prize by degrading them into worshipping of the holy angels, dwelling on the evidence of visions (see corrections, ch. ii. 18), and self-conceited, because not holding, and therefore not deriving strength from, the Head, the Lord Jesus Christ. This submission of theirs to be prescribed to by men is then further stigmatized. If they died to the world with Christ, why did they allow themselves to be debarred from the use of those things which Christ has cleansed for us, as though they were living in the world? Why did they tamely submit to commands not to touch, not to taste, not to handle? Why did they submit to prohibitions against marriage, and commands to abstain from meats? Such things are not of the essence of our spiritual life, but belong merely to this perishable condition, and will vanish with it: and these meddling and petty ordinances about them serve to exalt pretended doctors and teachers into a repute for wisdom and heroism, because of their volunteering more than is required, and appearing to be humble and self-denying—but are not God's appointed way of honouring our bodies, the instruments of His glory, nay, are all so many feedings of carnal vanity, under the guise of carnal mortification.

Such is the fervid and outspoken denunciation with which the great Apostle meets the ascetics and the ritualists in the Colossian church. Such is his protest on behalf of the life of Christian liberty, and Christian loftiness of aim and spirit. We can hardly conceive a more direct declaration of the apostolic mind on the controversies which in these our times agitate the Church of Christ. Do we want to know how one who thought, and as to whom we think, that he had the Spirit of God, regarded the observance of times, the abstinence from allowable states of life, or lawful sustenance of life? Come here and take his rule, not derived through ages of doctors and corruptors, but fresh from the fountain head. Do you want an instructive and a decisive contrast? Read first a page of the 'Directorium Anglicanum,' and then read Col. ii. 8-23, and say which is binding on us

Christians: for both cannot be. Was St. Paul 'an irreverent Dissenter'? Or are these chasubled gentlemen, these prescribers and proscribers, false churchmen? Because it does seem to me, that we must accept one or other of these alternatives.

Of course the passage is as strong a protest against the whole Romanist system, which is founded on, and upheld by, precisely the principles which St. Paul here impugns. If we have not mentioned that system first, it is partly because our present conflict, being with false teachers within a church which holds primitive truth, more nearly resembles that in our Epistle, than our protest against error outside our communion: but chiefly because Roman ritualism, as venerable and consistent, while we cannot approve it, commands our respect: Anglican, as the mere upstart caricature of the other, as inconsequent and suicidal, stands out prominent for the loathing and contempt of all honest men.

With ch. ii. the controversial part of our Epistle ends, and the hortatory begins. We were raised with Christ in our baptism: we must therefore live that heavenly resurrection-life which Christ is now living; for our life is hidden in Him, and our manifestation in glory will coincide with His manifestation. We should then be dead to the present world, its lusts and ambitions and strifes. To this mortification, and the corresponding new life after the image of God, he now exhorts them in detail. All are to be loving, pitiful, and forgiving : all are to praise God with the life and with the lips : all are to consecrate their whole lives to the service of their master, Jesus. And if all, then each separate class, out of which classes, put together, the community is made up : each glorifying God, each serving the Master Christ, in its peculiar place and circumstances : wives and husbands, children and parents, slaves and masters.

After this the letter concludes with a few private notices. Tychicus was to bear it to them, and to carry them news of the Apostle's state. With him was to go Onesimus, the once fugitive, but now penitent and returning slave: concerning whom we shall have more to say in our next chapter. Among those who send salutations we find one name of considerable interest to us. 'It is that of Mark, 'cousin (see corrections) to Barnabas.' Our readers will remember the last occasion on which this name came before us in the apostolic history. It was when Paul and Barnabas were divided asunder owing to the misconduct of this same Mark, and to the desire of his relative, notwithstanding, to take him with them on their missionary journey. It would appear that since then he had been received into favour by St. Paul, and had been the subject of a general order to the churches obeying St. Paul, that they should receive him. This Mark, or John Mark, is generally supposed to have been the writer of our second Gospel. The notices of him are very few, and on that account every scrap is interesting. We also find respecting him here, that he is classed with the small number of the Apostle's fellow-workers who had been a comfort to him. We have also a greeting here from 'Luke, the beloved physician,' the writer of the third Gospel. It is very possible that the expression, 'the beloved physician,' may be not without a meaning of some interest. It appears to have been after a serious illness of St. Paul, that St. Luke first became permanently attached to him as a companion (compare Gal. iv. 13, 14 with Acts xvi. 6—10), and we can hardly avoid surmising that the obligation of the Apostle to his fellow-traveller may have caused him to attach this appellation to his name. We have another mentioned here, of whom we shall hear again: Demas, whose stay with St. Paul was not permanent.

After these notices follow two directions: one, on which we have already remarked, that the Colossian and Laodicean churches should interchange the Epistles sent to them, and that each should be read in the church of the other; and another, a solemn charge to Archippus, probably the son of Philemon of Colossæ, to take heed of the ministry which he had received in the Lord, that he fulfil it. From this we may infer that he was a young man but recently admitted to holy orders. The Apostle adds a salutation in his own hand; the rest of the Epistle having been written by another hand at his dictation. He entreats them not to forget him in his imprisonment, to bear in mind the chain which moved over the paper as he wrote, and all the circumstances of bodily need and spiritual depression which it implied, and with the simple 'Grace be with you,' concludes.

The Epistle to the Colossians, while it takes a high rank among St. Paul's letters for fervour of rebuke and of affection, is less severe than that to the Galatians, and less affectionate than those to the Thessalonians and Philippians. It is one of those letters which spring out of an occasion, and mainly treat of it. So did that to the Galatians; and it is remarkable that each of the principal *occasional* Epistles of the Apostle gave rise to a greater general Epistle; the Galatian Epistle, to that to the Romans; this, to that to the Ephesians.

We have now to give our lists of corrections in reading and rendering. In doing so, we cannot help expressing our thankfulness that, as we learn from various letters, these lists are valued, and find their way into the margins of men's cottage Bibles. Of all the wants of the English Church, one of the greatest is a better version of the New Testament Epistles. The churches in Britain are not dealing honestly with this great matter. There are hundreds of learned clergymen, who know in their hearts that a revision is an absolute duty, but who dare not speak out. This being so, it is something to know that we have, in however humble a degree, contributed to deepen the public dissatisfaction with the present inadequate and over-praised version. But to our task. And first, as usual, for those corrections which are required to bring the text into accordance with the testimony of the most ancient manuscript authorities.

In ch. i. 3, 'God *and* the Father,' should be 'God the Father.' In ver. 6, instead of '*and bringeth forth fruit,*' read, 'it is bringing forth fruit and growing,'— placing a semicolon at 'world,' which precedes. In ver. 7, omit '*also;*' and instead of 'for *you,*' read, 'on our behalf.' In ver. 10, for '*in* the knowledge,' read 'by the knowledge.' In ver. 14, the words '*through his blood*' are not found in any of our ancient authorities, and should be expunged. They have been borrowed from Eph. i. 7, where they are genuine.

In ch. ii. 2, for 'the mystery of God, *and of the Father, and of Christ,*' read merely, 'the mystery of God.' The addition has probably taken place owing to the common practice of the writers of the MSS. of explaining in the margin, when the divine Name occurs, to which Person it belongs. Thus, 'of God' having been all that was in the original, 'the Father' would by one be put as a marginal explanation, 'Christ' by another: and then these notes would by subsequent transcribers be added to, or substituted for, that which was in the text. In the present place, there is great confusion in the additional words, even in the ancient MSS.; and, in that case, the shortest text is to be presumed to have been the original one. In ver. 11, '*the sins of*' should be expunged, not being found in any of our ancient authorities. In ver. 13, for '*you* all trespasses,' read 'us all trespasses.' In ver. 18, instead of 'things which he hath *not* seen,' read, 'things which he hath seen,' with the majority of our ancient authorities. See, on this place, the corrections of renderings below. In ver. 20, omit '*wherefore.*'

In ch. iii. 6, the verse which, as it now stands, has been conformed to Eph. v. 6, should be read thus:—'On which account cometh the wrath of God,' omitting the rest. In ver. 12, for '*mercies,*' read 'pity.' In ver. 13, for '*Christ,*' read 'the Lord;' and in ver. 15, for '*God,*' read '*Christ.*' In ver. 16, 'psalms *and* hymns *and*,' omit 'and' both times, and place commas—'psalms, hymns,' spiritual songs.' At the end of the verse, for '*the Lord,*' read 'God.' In ver. 17, for 'God *and* the

Father,' read 'God the Father.' In ver. 18, omit '*our*.' In ver. 20, for '*unto* the Lord,' read 'in the Lord.' In ver. 22, for 'the Lord,' read 'God;' and omit '*And*,' at the beginning of ver. 23. In ver. 24, instead of '*for ye serve* the Lord Christ,' read 'Serve ye the Lord Christ.' At the beginning of ver. 25, for '*But*,' read 'For.'

In ch. iv. 7, several of our oldest MSS. begin the verse as in Eph. vi. 22, 'That ye may know our state. . . .' But when passages are thus found conformed to one another, the *differing* reading, if at all worthily supported, is the true one. The tendency of transcribers always was to conform parallel places verbally to one another; sometimes from mere carelessness; afterwards, when the text of Scripture began to be regarded as verbally inspired, from superstitious motives. In ver. 12, for '*Christ*,'' read 'Christ Jesus;' and for '*complete*,' 'fully assured.' In ver. 13, for '*zeal*,' read 'labour.' At the end, omit 'Amen,' with most of our oldest MSS.

The corrections necessary owing to wrong or inadequate renderings are as follows:—

In ch. i. 11, render, 'being strengthened with all strength, according to the might of his glory.'

This is one those cases where the English translation unfortunately expresses by a mere adjective-epithet what is in the original the principal substantive. In verses 12, 13, omit '*hath*,' all three times. The reference is not to our present state, but to God's past act in each case. In ver. 14, '*redemption*' should be 'our redemption.' In ver. 15, '*every creature*' should be 'all creation.' In ver. 16, '*by* him' should be 'in him.' The difference is most important; and the 'in' of the original ought never to have been tampered with. As God in Christ reconciled the world to himself, so also God in Christ created all things. It *was* 'by Christ'; but the expression implies far more, and that English readers lose. At end of verse, for 'were,' read 'have been.' In ver. 17, '*consist*' would now be better understood, if it were 'subsist.' In ver. 18, for 'might have the pre-eminence,' read 'may be the first.' In ver. 19, the Greek has only 'Because he was well pleased that in him should all the fulness dwell.' In ver. 20 for 'by him,' read (both times) 'through him.' In ver. 21, read 'by your wicked works;' and in ver. 22, 'through his death.' In ver. 23, *have* heard, should be 'heard.' In ver. 25, for '*am* made,' and '*is* given,' 'was made,' and 'was given.' In ver. 26, for 'ages' and 'generations,' 'the ages' and 'the generations :' viz., all that have ever been. In ver. 27, for '*would* make known,' 'was pleased to make known:' and for 'Christ *in* you,' 'Christ among you.'

In ch. ii. 2, for '*acknowledgment*,' 'thorough knowledge.' In ver. 3, for '*in whom are hid all the treasures*,' substitute 'wherein are all the hidden treasures.' In ver. 6, for 'As ye *have* therefore received,' read 'As therefore ye received :' and for '*as ye have been taught*,' 'even as ye were taught.' In ver. 8, for *spoil* you,' read 'lead you captive :' and for '*philosophy*,' 'his philosophy.' In ver. 11, for '*in whom also ye are circumcised*,' 'in whom ye were also circumcised,' viz., at the time of your baptism: and the 'also' is connected, not with 'whom,' but with the verb. For '*the* circumcision,' 'a circumcision.' At end of verse for '*by* the circumcision of Christ,' 'in the circumcision of Christ.' In ver. 12, for '*baptism*,' 'your baptism :' for '*wherein also ye are risen*,' 'wherein ye were also raised :' for '*faith of*,' 'the faith in :' and for '*hath* raised,' 'raised.' In ver. 13, '*sins*' ought to be 'trespasses :' and '*hath* he quickened,' 'he quickened,' or 'did he quicken :' viz., at that same time. In ver. 14, '*took*,' should be 'hath taken:' and '*his* cross,' 'the cross.' The translators fancied that the *subject* of the whole sentence was Christ, whereas it is God the Father. In ver. 15, 'having spoiled,' should be 'stripping off from himself,' 'divesting himself of': *i.e.* in the cross of Christ God put off from himself the ministration of angels, by which the law was given, subjecting them all to Christ, whose triumph they grace, as we also are said to do, 2 Cor. ii. 14 (see corrected rendering there). Therefore, angels were no more to be regarded as mediators between God and man, nor the law which they ministered, as binding. Thus, and rendering 'the principalities and the powers' (viz., the same as those before spoken of in ver. 10, and ch. i. 16, and Eph. iii. 10), the connexion with the next verse becomes plain, which in the authorised version is totally obscured. At end, for '*in him*,' read 'in it,' **viz.**, the cross. In ver. 16, for 'in *meat* or in *drink*,' read 'in eating or in drinking.' 'An *holyday*' would now be better understood, if it were 'a feast day.' Omit '*the*' before 'Sabbath days:' the Apostle's command extends further than to the *Jewish* Sabbath only. In ver. 17, for '*things*,' 'the things.' Read ver. 18

thus: 'Let no one of purpose defraud you of your prize, in lowliness of mind and worshipping of the angels, insisting on things which he hath seen' (see corrections of reading above). In ver. 20, for '*if ye be dead*,' 'if ye died.' For '*are ye subject to ordinances*,' 'are ye (do ye suffer yourselves to be) prescribed to.' In ver. 23, for '*will worship*,' read 'voluntary worship:' for '*humility*,' 'lowliness of mind:' for '*neglecting*,' 'not sparing:' and place a comma at 'honour,' thus connecting the last clause with what went before, not with the word 'honour.'

In ch. iii. 1, for '*be risen*,' read 'were raised.' In ver. 2, '*affection*' should be 'mind.' The Greek is merely 'mind the things,' &c. Read, both times, 'the things.' In ver. 3, '*are dead*' ought to be 'died.' In ver. 4, '*shall appear*' ought to be 'is manifested,' and '*appear*' the second time, 'be manifested.' In ver. 5, '*mortify*' conveys no meaning to the modern English ear. It is, 'kill,' or 'make dead.' '*Inordinate affection*' should be 'lustful passion.' In ver. 8, 'put off' is imperative, which no English reader would suspect. Read it, 'But now lay ye also aside the whole.' *Filthy communication*' is what we now call 'foul language.' In ver. 10, for 'is removed,' 'is being removed:' the verb is *present*, and the act is going on, not completed. For '*in knowledge*,' 'unto the perfect knowledge.' In ver. 11, for '*neither*,' better 'no such thing as;' and it ought to be 'Greek and Jew,' 'circumcision and uncircumcision:' not '*nor*' in each case. The meaning actually conveyed by the English version is, that in Christ there are *no Greeks nor Jews, no circumcised nor uncircumcised, no Barbarians, Scythians, bond nor freemen:* whereas the Apostle says that there is no *such thing as* 'Greek and Jew,' *i.e.* the distinction between them. The last four have no copula: and should stand, 'barbarian, Scythian, bondman, freeman.' In ver. 14, '*above* all these things' does not mean 'more especially than all these things:' but above *in position*, on top of. Better therefore read 'over all these things.' For '*charity*,' read 'love.' In ver. 15, '*are* called' should be 'were called.' In ver. 16, put the *semicolon before* the words 'in all wisdom:' they belong to 'teaching,' &c., which follows. In ver. 19, for '*bitter*,' read 'embittered:' not only be not bitter, but do not allow yourselves to be worked up to wrath against them. In ver. 21, 'disheartened' is better than '*discouraged*.' In ver. 23, '*do* it' should be, 'work at it.' In ver.

25. '*receive for* the wrong' should be, 'receive back the wrong.'

In ch. iv. 3, '*of utterance*' should be 'for the word.' In ver. 5, '*redeeming the times*' should be. 'buying up opportunities' (see the explanation in our future remarks on Eph. v. 16). In ver. 10. '*sister's son*' ought to be 'cousin.' In ver. 17, for '*hast received*,' read '*receivedst.*'

X.

THE EPISTLE TO PHILEMON.

THIS short letter differs from all others which have come down to us as parts of the canon of Scripture. It gives us a glimpse of the private friendships of an apostle, and of the social intercourse which he held with his fellow Christians. And this, in relation to a matter originally of mere private interest: the return and reception of a runaway slave. If it be asked, what motive can have led to the placing of such a letter among the books of Scripture, we Christians have no hesitation to Whose guidance to ascribe its preservation. It cannot have been thus honoured merely as a relic of St. Paul; for there must have been scores of similar letters in the possession of men and families in the early Christian world, which, had that primitive age been as careful of relics as we are now taught to believe it was, would have been preserved with equal care. All these others have perished, and this only remains. I believe that reason sufficient will appear, before the conclusion of our present paper, why this should have been so; that the instruction to be derived from this private letter concerning a mere domestic matter, will vindicate itself as thoroughly worthy to have been conserved for the church in all ages.

First, let us review the circumstances under which the epistle was written. And here let me say that, wishing to make this chapter complete in itself, I shall not be careful to avoid repeating information given already in the preceding chapter, on the Epistle to the Colossians. The reader will thank me for sparing him the troublesome task of referring back and combining the two accounts.

During St. Paul's long sojourn of three whole whole years at Ephesus, the principal city of Asia Minor, he appears to have become the founder of several churches in that country, without having himself visited the towns where they sprung up. The general expression in the narrative in the Acts is, that "*all that dwelt in Asia heard the word of God, both Jews and Greeks;*" and in Col. ii. 1, the

Apostle speaks of the people of Colossæ and Laodicea as never having seen his face in the flesh. It is to the first mentioned of these, Colossæ, that our attention is now directed. It had once been an important city, but had a few years before the time of which we are speaking been desolated by a terrible earthquake, from the effects of which it appears never afterwards to have recovered. During St. Paul's stay at Ephesus, Epaphras, an inhabitant of Colossæ, became acquainted with him, and received from his lips the word of truth, which became the seed of the Colossian church. Probably in consequence of this, others from the town visited the Apostle, and among them the family with whom we are now concerned, consisting of Philemon; Apphia, his wife; Archippus, probably their son; and Onesimus, their slave. The result of the intercourse between them was that the head of the family became a missionary to his native town—a fellow labourer with the Apostle. Apphia became a sister in Christ; and Archippus, apparently at that time a youth, was afterwards admitted to holy orders; for in the Epistle to the Colossians, iv. 17, St. Paul writes, 'Say unto Archippus, Take heed to the ministry which thou receivedst in the Lord, that thou fulfil it.'

We must now pass over six or seven years. In that interval, the Apostle has gone through all those trials and perils which signalised the latter portion of his missionary journeyings as related in the Acts: has stood before Felix and Festus; and, having for his safety used his right as a Roman citizen of appealing to Cæsar, has been sent prisoner to Rome. He is dwelling there under military custody in his own hired house, resorted to by Christian brethren from all parts of the East. Among the rest comes Epaphras, with news of a mixed kind from Colossæ—news which, making the Apostle both joyful and anxious, set him upon despatching at once an epistle thither. Two messengers are with him, ready to be the bearers of his letter. One of these was Tychicus, a native of Asia, and companion of St. Paul on his missionary journeys. On the other we will for a new minutes direct our attention. He is no other than the slave Onesimus, of whom we before said that he had probably accompanied his master, Philemon, to Ephesus, and there had become acquainted with St. Paul. So much is, I think, necessary to be supplied in order to account for what we find now happening. Onesimus has become since then a runaway from his master. He has escaped the search of the slave-police, established expressly for the purpose of tracking and bringing back fugitives, and is lying hid, where all that was bad and disreputable found its confluence and its concealment, in the great metropolis, Rome. There, led by what providential chance we know not, he visits the Apostle. He may have been brought by Epaphras. More probably he may have recollected, with fond regret, amongst the refuse of the lowest society, in which such a fugitive would naturally be found, the pure and warm-hearted man who had wrought such a change in his master's family—who had reasoned, in his case in vain, of righteousness, temperance, and judgment to come. He may have been not unacquainted with some part of the Apostle's subsequent course. He may have even worked his way in one of the ships in which St. Paul had made his broken and perilous voyage to Rome. Or he may have accidentally heard that he was now a prisoner in the same city. Be this as it may, the two met together; the runaway slave, the Apostle of Christ,—and the result of the meeting was that the slave became a Christian brother. The guilt of an accusing conscience, the sense of insecurity and danger, the ties of reviving affection and gratitude drawing him back to his master, all pleaded on the side of the Apostle, and Onesimus was convinced. As in Hagar's case, so in this, so in every case of forsaken duty, the voice of God's messenger is, 'Return and submit thyself.' At whatever cost or risk, the first work of the penitent must be to repair as far as possible the wrong done. So Onesimus is ready to start from Rome on his way back to his master at Colossæ. Naturally such a traveller would seek for a letter of commendation. He would be afraid of the anger of his master, even were that master a Christian brother; and we are, I think, almost compelled to assume, from the deprecatory tone of this letter, that Philemon was a master from whom severity was to be expected. Paul the aged, from whom both his master and he had received the glad tidings of salvation, would, if any could, be an effectual pleader for him. So the Apostle dictates, and partly, or even perhaps wholly, writes with his own hand such a letter as Onesimus required—a letter containing nothing respecting church doctrine and discipline, but wholly concerning this one private matter, praying earnestly that the returned slave might be kindly received, and his former faults forgiven; mentioning the happy change which had taken place in him during his flight, and bespeaking for him on his return, not only a welcome, but recognition as a Christian brother. And thus the Church has acquired this letter. It was preserved in the family to which it was addressed, and read first, no doubt, as a precious apostolic message of love and blessing, in the church which assembled in Philemon's house. Then copies of it became multiplied, and from Colossæ it spread through the church universal. It is quoted as early as the end of the second century, and has ever, except with some few who question everything, remained an undoubted portion of the writings of St. Paul.

Let us now examine the Epistle, for our understanding and use. The Apostle begins it by calling himself '*a prisoner of Jesus Christ.*' This he did not do in the opening of the letter to the Colossians, which was written and sent at the same time. There, associating with himself Timothy, as here, and by the same title of '*our brother,*' he calls himself '*an apostle;*' here, '*a prisoner.*' Doubtless this was because there he wished to carry the weight of authority: here, he is requesting a favour. This view is substantiated by our finding him by and by, ver. 9, when he is about to prefer his petition, mentioning this fact of his being 'a prisoner' of Jesus Christ, as an additional reason why it should be kindly received. When he is beseeching the Ephesians to walk worthily of the vocation wherewith they were called, he similarly styles himself '*the prisoner of the Lord.*'

He addresses the letter, coupling Timothy with himself, to the whole household of Philemon, and to the church that is in his house. There is a certain tact and skill in this. Some of us might think that in a matter regarding the treatment of a servant by his master, that master only ought to have been exhorted, and by one person only: but when, by thus joining another with Himself, and others in the house to Philemon, he makes them witnesses of a jointly-given counsel, he gently reminds Philemon, that even our domestic duties are not matters of which we may judge by ourselves, and purely as regards ourselves, but that as to them also we owe an obligation to the feelings of one another, to our own families, and to the church of God. He also skilfully provides for the success of his exhortations: for if Philemon might have been tempted to treat lightly advice of which only he himself was cognizant, he hardly could, consistently with his wish to stand well with those about him, do so when others also were aware of it.

A word respecting this *church in Philemon's house.* Remember that this was before there were any fixed buildings appropriated to purposes of divine worship. The Christians assembled where and how they could, and generally, we may well suppose, in not very large numbers: and thus the house of the minister, or of some other Christian brother, became a regular place of meeting for prayer and the sacrament. We learn from the Epistle to the Colossians that in the neighbouring city of Laodicea one Nymphas similarly assembled the church in his house: and in Rom. xvi. 5, and 1 Cor. xvi. 19, the same is said of Aquila and Priscilla. '*Where do you assemble?*' the heathen prefect asked of the primitive apostolic father, Justin Martyr. 'Where each one can and will,' was the answer. 'You believe, no doubt, that we all meet together in one place; but it is not so, for the God of the Christians is not shut up in a room, but He fills heaven and earth, and is honoured everywhere by the faithful.' He adds, in relating this, that he himself had ordinarily such an assembly in his own house. The practice is interesting, as showing the independence of our holy religion on outward circumstances : but it is not to be quoted in disparagement of our present practice. When the circumstances of the Church altered, her practice also altered. She is the Church of all time, and of every land ; and is no more obliged to continue, in these times, her primitive modes of assembling, than they were to anticipate our fashion.

The Apostle proceeds to pave the way for his coming request, by commending the faith and love of him to whom he was writing. Philemon had refreshed the hearts of the saints; was known as one full of benevolence and Christian charity. This, the Apostle says, made him the bolder. He might have *commanded* him to do what was fitting ; this also he mentions to bespeak acceptance for the lesser thing—viz., his request for love's sake.

And thus he introduces the subject of his letter, even further bespeaking favour for it by the circumstance of his being now Paul the aged, and in chains for Jesus' sake. Onesimus is his own child; a birth into the Christian Church, which had been the fruit of his own imprisonment. His name ONESIMUS, in Greek, signified 'profitable;' little indeed had this signification as yet been verified; but now the unprofitable one had become a source of profit—to the Apostle, whose ministry he had sealed,—to his master, who would receive him now not as a slave, a chattel, but as a brother beloved. The Apostle had a thought of retaining him to minister to himself that duty which he gently reminds Philemon that he, the master, owed to his father in the faith; but he is unwilling to take his service for granted, and thus constrain it; all that he does for the Apostle shall be of free will.

The pleader now becomes more pressing, and assumes a more serious tone. Perhaps there was another hand in all this; perhaps it was of God, whose providence had deprived him of a servant for a season, to bestow upon him a friend and brother eternally. And so, if he counted St. Paul as a fellow-labourer, he was to receive Onesimus as he would receive himself.

But one thing remained. Since a slave could possess nothing, the means of escape and sustenance must have been fraudulently obtained out of his master's property, even supposing there was no greater theft behind. To whatever sum this damage amounted, St. Paul gives his word that he would himself be chargeable with it. His own hand attests this, whether he wrote this portion only, or, as is more probable, the whole letter, himself. But he does not expect this his pledge to be redeemed. He delicately reminds Philemon that a far greater debt is owing to him than can be due from him—'*even thine own self*'—to him who first taught thee the worth of thine own soul. This being so, let me have profit of thee (another allusion to the name of Onesimus), not indeed in worldly good, but in a rich increase of voluntary compliance over and above my present request.

Thus (and who shall say that it is discourteously or unskilfully?) he urges his plea, and concludes by holding out a prospect of a visit to them, and by sending salutations from those who were with him. All is closed with the benediction, '*The grace of our Lord Jesus Christ be with your spirit.*'

And now let us gather up the thoughts which we may carry away from this short epistle.

First, it furnishes an important evidence of the

apostolic spirit, or, which is for us the same thing, the teaching of the Spirit of God, with regard to a subject much debated, but now, by God's good Providence, happily determined in our time—I mean *slavery*. We learn from this letter two things. 1. That the Apostle will not rashly or hastily interfere with existing institutions. He had elsewhere advised (1 Cor. vii. 20) that every man should abide in the calling in which he finds himself; and had recommended the Christian slave, even if he might be free, rather to continue as he was (v. 21). And here he is consistent with himself. He never requests Philemon to set Onesimus free, but only to receive him back kindly.

So much for one side. But we must not lose sight of the other. It has been often and well observed that, though St. Paul was no abolitionist, yet St. Paul's principles, if carried out, inevitably lead to the abolition of slavery. The gentleness which he here recommends, and elsewhere enjoins, coupled with the great doctrine which he never ceases to enforce, of the union of all mankind in Christ, could not make way among men, without the institution of slavery falling before them. The best practical proof of this is, that as these have made way, slavery *has* fallen. So then let us be fair. Let us not quote the moderation of the Apostle on the one side, without remembering that all the weight of his principles and character was thrown, and has prevailed, on the other.

Secondly, we happen to possess the means of comparing this specimen of Christian intercession with a like specimen from the pen of a kindly-spirited and cultivated heathen. The younger Pliny, the same who wrote the celebrated letter to the Emperor Trajan about the Christians in Bithynia, writes to his friend Sabinianus entreating his pardon for a freedman who had offended him; and writes again, acknowledging gratefully the granting of his request. The letters are models of courtesy, humanity, good feeling. But to a Christian mind, the comparison with this of St. Paul is most instructive. They lack just that in which this is eminent. Pliny conjures his friend by motives of pity, of self-respect, even of self-indulgence, for, says he, anger must be a torment to a man of your benevolent disposition. Nay, he puts in another motive still:—if you spare him now, you will have more excuse for anger with him in case he offends hereafter. Paul writes to his friend far otherwise.

There is no mere appeal to pity, no mirror held up to self-esteem, no afterthoughts admitting and justifying inconsistency: all comes warm from the loving heart, and all the heart's love is kindled by the love of Christ.

Thirdly, we have here the instructive sight of a man practising what he has preached. Some years before, St. Paul wrote the beautiful description of love in 1 Cor. xiii. Now many a man may write a beautiful description, and yet not exemplify it in his own conduct. Sometimes sympathy, sometimes enthusiasm, sometimes mere pride, makes us orators—makes us angels; but when we are off our prophesying chairs, the old Adam prevails, and we falsify our own words. It is a pleasing glimpse into St. Paul's character, when we see that this was not so with him. The love which he eulogized then, he exhibits now. Where can we find a nobler illustration of the beautiful words, 'Love is long-suffering, is kind; love envieth not; love vaunteth not itself, is not puffed up, doth not behave itself unseemly, seeketh not its own, is not easily provoked, imputeth not the evil; rejoiceth not at unrighteousness, but rejoiceth at the truth; beareth all things, believeth all things, hopeth all things, endureth all things'? Here was a prisoner with a chain clanking on his arm, with anxiety about his own fate continually gnawing his heart, with the constant presence of an alien keeper, the eyes ever fixed on him, which have been described* as the greatest torture of guarded imprisonment; with the care of all the churches upon him, and the endless complications of relations of Jew and Gentile to arrange,—yet finding room in his heart for the poor runaway slave, and time and words at his command to plead his cause. Such, we may add, is the grace of God's Holy Spirit; such the power of holy love; such the bloom of Christian courtesy and Christian humility.

Again, the history of Onesimus himself is not without its instruction and consolation for us. Like the prodigal, he had fled from his home, and amidst the secret haunts of the depraved metropolis was seeking concealment from justice. But even there the messenger of grace and mercy found him, and he was restored, not to his former estate, but to far greater blessedness: he found, not only a reconciled master on earth, but a loving and precious Master in heaven. Many, in commenting on this

* See 'The Prison Life of Jefferson Davis.'

Epistle, have reminded us of the deeper thought which has occurred to them, that St. Paul is indeed here our example, but was himself following a higher example; even that of Him who found *us* wandering from our duty and our Father's house, and pleaded for *our restoration* with His own suffering, and His own most precious blood.

But beyond doubt, *the* lesson of all others from this Epistle is, that we should carry into the concerns of private life the courtesy and the Christian spirit here shown by the Apostle; that we should talk to one another, argue with one another, write letters to one another, not as men of the world, but as disciples of Christ; not as Pliny, but as St. Paul; remembering Whose we are, and Whom we serve; and that our religion is to be a light shining before men, to show forth the glory of Him who hath redeemed us by Christ.

Our usual task of summing up the necessary corrections of readings and renderings, will in this case be naturally but a short one.

In ver. 2, instead of '*our beloved Apphia,*' read, with all our oldest MSS., 'Apphia our sister.' In ver. 4, our three oldest MSS. omit '*Jesus*.' In the same verse, for '*you*,' read 'us,' with all our oldest

MSS. In ver. 7, for '*we have*,' read 'I had.' In ver. 12, for '*sent again*,' read 'sent back to thee.' In the same verse, omit 'thou therefore.' In ver. 20, for '*the Lord*,' read 'Christ.'

As to corrections in the rendering: in ver. 4, it should stand, 'I thank my God always, making mention of thee in my prayers.' And in the next verse, 'hearing of thy love, and of the faith which thou hast,' &c. 'All *the* saints,' should be, 'all saints.' In ver. 6, render, 'may become effectual unto Christ in the knowledge of every good thing which is in us.' In ver. 7, and also in vers. 12 and 20, 'heart' expresses much better that which '*bowels*' was intended to convey. In ver. 7, for '*are* refreshed,' read 'have been refreshed.' In ver. 8, for 'though I *might be* much bold,' read 'though I have much boldness;' and for '*convenient*,' 'fitting.' Place the period at the former 'beseech thee,' and connect the next words with what follows: 'Being such an one,—as Paul the aged, and now also a prisoner of Christ Jesus,— I beseech thee,' &c. In ver. 9, '*son*' should be 'child,' and 'have begotten' should be 'begat.' In ver. 13, for '*would have retained*,' read 'was purposing to retain;' and for '*might have ministered*,' 'might minister.' In ver. 14, for '*benefit*,' read 'good service.' In ver. 15, for '*shouldest* receive him,' 'mayest receive him.' In ver. 19, for '*albeit I do not say*,' 'that I say not.' In ver. 20, for '*joy*,' read 'profit;' the word is a play on the name '*Onesimus*.' In ver. 21, for '*wrote*,' 'have written;' and for '*wilt also do more*,' 'wilt do even more.' In ver. 22, for '*withal*,' read 'at the same time.'

Our next chapter will be on the Epistle to the Ephesians; which, being written and sent at the same time, and by the same messenger, as those to the Colossians and Philemon, as well as from its internal similarity to the former of those Epistles, naturally enters into the same group with them.

XI.

THE EPISTLE TO THE EPHESIANS.

IN the consideration of this great Epistle, we are at once met by a question which it is of some consequence satisfactorily to answer. There has been in all ages a doubt, whether its present title is rightly given. In order to deal with this, for the general reader, we must first explain its grounds.

It will be remembered that St. Paul had spent a portion of time which he himself describes as 'three whole years' at Ephesus. He was bound to the church there by ties of the closest affection, as appears by the pathetic description of the leave-taking in Acts xx. He writes, as commonly reputed, an Epistle to that church. Yet in it do we find not one single instance of personal greeting, so common in his other Epistles. Is this probable?

Secondly, it is said that in this Epistle the conversion of those to whom it was addressed is stated to have been known to the writer only by report (ch. i. 15), which could not be likely, considering that he founded the Ephesian church himself.

Thirdly, he seems to treat his readers' knowledge of himself as an Apostle, as one accruing by hearsay only, — so that he needed credentials to assure his mission to them (ch. iii. 2—4).

Fourthly, he describes, it is said, his readers as almost exclusively Gentiles (ch. ii. 11; iv. 17), and as having been but recently converted (ch. v. 8; i. 13; ii. 13).

Fifthly, the words 'in Ephesus' (ch. i. 1) are omitted by our most ancient MSS., and thus not only internal, but external, grounds exist for doubting whether the Epistle could have been addressed originally to the Ephesians.

We will deal with these somewhat formidable queries one by one.

As to the first then, we must be familiar with the Apostle's manner in sending his private salutations, before we can reply. 'They are found in greatest abundance in the Epistle to the Romans, written to a church which, as a church, he had never seen, but which, owing to its situation, contained many of his own friends and fellow-labourers, also many friends of those who were with him at Corinth. In 1 Corinthians, written to a church which he had founded, and where he had long resided (Acts xviii. 11), there is not one person saluted by name, and one salutation only sent,—from Aquila and Priscilla. In 2 Corinthians, not one personal salutation of either kind.' The Philippians were his 'dearly beloved, his joy, and his crown:' yet not one of them is saluted. The Galatians were his 'little children, of whom he was in labour till Christ should be formed in them:' yet not one is saluted. The Thessalonians were 'imitators of him and of the Lord, patterns to all that believed in Macedonia and Achaia:' yet not one of them is selected for salutation. What is even more to the point, Timothy was sent *to Ephesus* itself: yet in it no one is saluted. It is plain then, that we can infer nothing from this absence of salutations. He sometimes omits them when writing to intimate friends: he inserts them when writing to those whom he had never seen. The seriousness of his subject, or the mere play of his free feeling at the time, influenced him, and no merely local considerations. That this letter contains no personal salutations, is absolutely no reason why it should not have been addressed to the Ephesian church.

The second and third objections are entirely unfounded. He does not speak of knowing them, or their history, by report, but only their present state of faith and love, or rather, some notable instances of both which were 'among' them. And he does not say that they knew him only by report, or that he wanted credentials to them. This will appear in our corrections further on.

As to the fourth, he is elsewhere in the habit of addressing mixed churches as Gentiles (see 1 Cor. xii. 2), when their location was in the Gentile world. And of all Epistles this would be least likely to preserve the distinction, seeing that he is treating of the constitution and glories of the universal church. At the same time, there are not wanting indications of the mixed composition of the church to which he was writing: as in the words, 'that he might make the two into one new man in Himself' (ch. ii. 15).

To the latter part of this objection we may reply, that he uses the same term to express the

ngth of time since their conversion, as he uses
especting his own: compare Eph. ii. 13, v. 8,
with Gal. i. 13, 23; Titus iii. 3; so that no inference as to its recent occurrence can be drawn.

The fact that the words 'in Ephesus' are wanting in some ancient MSS., we may notice, (1) that
Basil, who observes upon this omission, yet regards
the Epistle addressed to the Ephesians; (2) that
the words 'in Rome' (Rom. i. 7) are also absent
from some MSS.; and that the local designation
appears to have been left out in order to generalise
the reference of the contents, when the subject
was one of catholic interest.

Some have supposed that our Epistle is that
spoken of Col. iv. 16, as to be got from Laodicea,
and read at Colossæ. But this is pure hypothesis.
No MS. substitutes the words 'in Laodicea' for
'in Ephesus.'

Others have believed that it was a kind of
circular letter addressed to various churches, and
to be designated as it might happen, a gap being
left to be filled in accordingly, 'in Ephesus,' 'in
Laodicea,' 'in Hierapolis,' &c. This view is even
more untenable than the other. The Epistle is
evidently addressed to one set of persons, co-

existing in one place, as one body, and under the same circumstances. No indication is found of this *encyclical* character as in 2 Corinthians and Galatians. For these, and for other reasons which I have treated in my 'Introduction to the New Testament for English Readers,' I have no hesitation in rejecting altogether this latter hypothesis.

We infer then, that the Epistle was veritably written, as now addressed, to the Ephesian church, and to no other.

Of that church let us now speak. Ephesus was a place of great commerce and note, at the mouth of the river Caÿster in Lydia. It was famed for its great temple of Diana, one of the wonders of the ancient world (Acts xix. 24, &c.). St. Paul's first and short visit to it is recorded Acts xviii. 19—21. The work begun by him was afterwards carried on by Apollos, and by Aquila and Priscilla. During his second visit, lasting 'three years,' he founded the Ephesian church (see Acts xix., xx.). The number of converts seems to have been considerable, and the church had been an especial object of the Apostle's personal care. On his last recorded journey to Jerusalem he did not touch at Ephesus, but summoned the elders of the Ephe-

sian church to meet him at Miletus, where he took
an affecting farewell of them, which at the time he
believed to be his last.

The subsequent history of this church will come
before us when we write on the first Epistle to
Timothy.

It is interesting, among the doubts which have
been above dealt with, to trace some minor indications, confirming the view that the Ephesian
church was that really addressed.

In St. Paul's farewell speech, Acts xx. 24, we
find him speaking of having preached to them the
'gospel of the grace of God,' and (ver. 32) com-
mitting them 'to the word of His grace.' It is,
therefore, interesting to notice that in this Epistle
alone, and not in the contemporary and similar
one to the Colossians, he uses such expressions
as 'the glory of His grace' (i. 6); 'the riches of
His grace' (i. 7, ii. 7); and that 'grace' in many
combinations runs through the whole letter. If he
preached among them 'the good tidings of the
grace of God,' this may well be called 'the Epistle
of the grace of God.'

In Acts xx. 22, he had said, 'I go *bound* in the
Spirit to Jerusalem.' .... '*Bonds* and afflictions

await me.' Accordingly, here alone, in his letters to churches, does he call himself 'the Lord's bondsman,' or 'prisoner' (chap. iii. 1; iv. 1).

In his speech in the Acts (xx. 28), he had said of the church of God, 'which He purchased with His own blood.' In Eph. i. 14, we have the singular expression, 'the redemption of the purchased possession.'

In Acts xx. 32, he commits them to God and the word of His grace, 'which was able to build them up, and give them an inheritance among the saints.' The image of *building*, often found elsewhere, is more than ever common in this Epistle; some have supposed in allusion to the great temple of Diana. But, however this may be, we can hardly fail to connect the words just quoted with Eph. i. 18, 'which is the riches of the glory of this inheritance among the saints;' i. 14, 'which is the earnest of our inheritance:' and v. 5, 'hath no inheritance in the kingdom of Christ and of God' (see Acts xix. 8).

When we come to inquire into the occasion of the Epistle, we find nothing special in the state of the Ephesian church which may account for it. Rather does it seem to have sprung out of the

circumstances of the Apostle's employment at
the time. He was sending, by Tychicus and Onesimus, a weighty letter to the Colossian church,
occasioned by defects in its belief and practice.
His mind was much exercised on the points which
he had to treat in that Epistle. But these very
matters were parts of a larger and more complete
subject, which the special import of that letter
would not allow him to introduce. He longed to
set forth the length and breadth and height of the
Church of Christ, as founded in the counsel of
the Father's will, wrought by the obedience and
love of the Son, carried on and nourished by the
indwelling influence of the Spirit. And to whom
could such an Epistle be addressed, but to that
Church which, more than any other, he had founded
and built up,—the church at Ephesus? This then
seems to be its occasion. It is to the Epistle to
the Colossians, what the Epistle to the Romans is
to that to the Galatians: a great offspring, greater
than the parent, embracing the general subject
of which the other treated a particular portion. He
addresses the Ephesian church as a type, a sample,
of the church universal. He sets forth to them
the *ground*, the *course*, the *aim and end* of the

church universal. All through the letter this threefold division is found. The *origin* of the church in the *will of the* FATHER; the *course* of the church by the *satisfaction of the* SON; the scope and aim of the church, *life in the* SPIRIT,—these three things run through the whole, dividing the Epistle first into three larger portions, and then in those portions carrying out the same order in every paragraph, and almost in every sentence. The whole is a magnificent apostolic comment on the doctrine of the Holy Trinity, as the divine Persons are concerned in the work of our redemption. Those who deny that doctrine, must either set aside this Epistle altogether, or must tear out of it all meaning and coherence. We shall presently have occasion to trace the design throughout the contents of the Epistle; meantime we will speak of its place and time of writing, as pointed out in its own pages.

These are easily traced by two indications. First, St. Paul was a *prisoner* when he wrote the Epistle, as appears from ch. iii. 1; iv. 1; vi. 20. This he was at Cæsarea (Acts xxi. 27—xxvi. 32) during parts of the years 58—60 A.D.: and at Rome, from the beginning of 61 to the end of the history in the Acts, and perhaps longer. Of these two periods, some have believed that the former was that of his writing this Epistle. I have, in my 'New Testament for English Readers,' examined the grounds of this opinion, and have found it far more probable that the Roman imprisonment, not the Cæsarean, was the time, as commonly believed. The free intercourse between him and others—the names of his associates who were with him at the time when the three Epistles were written—the interval which naturally separates the Epistle from the last visit, corresponding to the Roman imprisonment, but not to the Cæsarean — all these considerations tell very strongly for the common opinion. And if this be adopted, the time of writing will be fixed somewhere about the year 62 A.D.

In style and language, this Epistle is by far the most difficult of all St. Paul's writings. I have described it as follows in the work referred to above : —' Elsewhere, as in the Epistles to the Romans, Galatians, and Colossians, the difficulties lie for the most part at or near the surface : a certain degree of study will master, not indeed the mysteries of redemption which are treated of, but the coherence of the context, and the course of argument: or if not so, will at least serve to point out to every reader where the hard texts lie, and to bring out into relief each point with which he has to deal: whereas here, the difficulties lie altogether beneath the surface: are not discernible by the cursory reader, who finds all very straightforward and simple. All on the surface is smooth, and flows on unquestioned: but when we begin to inquire why thought succeeds to thought, and one cumbrous parenthesis to another — depths under depths disclose themselves, wonderful systems of parallel allusion, frequent and complicated under-plots: every word, the more we search, approves itself as set in its exact logical place: we see every phrase contributing, by its own similar organization and articulation, to the carrying out the organic whole. But this result is not won without much labour of thought—without repeated and minute laying together of portions and expressions—without bestowing on single words and phrases, and their succession and arrangement, as much study as would suffice for whole sections of those Epistles which carry their meaning more on the surface.'

We will now follow the Apostle's great subject through the Epistle.

After the customary apostolic greeting, begins the first portion of the Epistle, i. 3—iii. 21—THE DOCTRINE OF THE CHURCH OF CHRIST. This is subdivided as follows:—

I. The Ground and Origin of the Church, in the FATHER'S counsel, and His act in Christ, by the Spirit, i. 3—23. In carrying out this, the Apostle gives (1.) the preliminary idea of the church, set forth in the form of an ascription of praise, i. 3—14, and thus arranged:—The FATHER, in His eternal love, has chosen us unto holiness (ver. 4), ordained us to sonship (ver. 5), bestowed grace on us in the Beloved (ver. 6): in the SON, we have —redemption through the riches of His grace (ver. 7), knowledge of the mystery of His will (ver. 8, 9), inheritance under Him as the one Head (ver. 10 —12); through the SPIRIT we are sealed, by hearing the word of salvation (ver. 13), by receiving the earnest of our inheritance (ver. 14), until the redemption of the purchased possession (*ibid.*) (2.) The idea of the church carried forward, in the form of a prayer for the Ephesians, in which the fulfilment of the Father's counsel through the Son, by the Spirit, in his people, is set forth as consisting in the knowledge of the hope of his calling, of the riches of his promise, and the power which He exercises on His saints as first wrought by Him in Christ, whom He has made Head over all to the church.

II. The Course and Progress of the Church through the SON (ii. 1—22) : thus subdivided : (1.) ver. 1—10, the power of the Father in quickening us, both Gentiles and Jews, in and with Christ (ver. 1—6); his purpose in manifesting this power (ver. 7); inference respecting the method of our salvation (ver. 10). (2.) ver. 11—22, hortatory expansion of the foregoing into detail; reminding them what they once were (ver. 11, 12); what they now were in Christ (ver. 13—22).

III. The Aim and End of the Church in the SPIRIT (iii. 1—21) mainly set forth in the revelation to it of the mystery of Christ, through the ministry, working in the Spirit; and primarily, as regarded these Ephesians, by himself. Thus (1.) of his office as Apostle of the Gentiles (ver. 1—13) ; (2.) under the form of a prayer for them, of the aim and end of that office as respected the church; its becoming strong in the power of the Spirit (ver. 14—19).

Then (ver. 20, 21) a doxology concludes this first portion of the Epistle.

Now begins THE SECOND PORTION OF THE EPISTLE, being *hortatory* (iv. 1—vi. 20): and herein—

I. (iv. 1—16) The ground of the Christian's duties as a member of the church, viz., the unity of the mystical body of Christ (ver. 1—6), the manifoldness of grace given to each (ver. 7—13), that we may come to perfection in Him (ver. 14—16).

II. (iv. 17—vi. 9) Exhortations to a course of walking and conversation, derived from the ground just laid down. And herein (1.) (iv. 17—v. 21), general duties of Christians as united to Christ their Head: (2.) (v. 22—vi. 9) the Christian duties being all thus comprehended and hallowed by the church, the Apostle treats of them in the three greatest of the social relations: that of husband and wife (v. 22—33), that of parent and child (vi. 1—4), that of master and servant (vi. 5—9).

Then the Epistle draws to a conclusion, in a general exhortation to the spiritual conflict and to prayer (vi. 10—20): that conclusion itself being introduced by the announcement of the mission of Tychicus with the Epistle (vi. 21, 22), and completed with the apostolic blessing (vi. 23, 24).

It is well that the reader should have his attention called to the fact, and the nature, of the similarities between this Epistle and that to the Colossians. No one who reads with any intelligent attention can fail to have observed them; and few but will have seen how probable it is that a writer sending two letters at the same time should cast the two in the same common mould. If the one were written under special circumstances, while the other was intended as a more general exposition of the writer's mind, then would this common form be modified to suit those circumstances in the one case, and not in the other.

Now this is precisely what we find in the two Epistles. It is not our purpose to compare them throughout; but let any reader take the two first chapters of each, paragraph by paragraph, and see for himself whether it be not so.

'In writing both, the Apostle's mind was in the same general frame—full of the glories of the person of Christ, and the consequent glorious privileges of his church, which is built on Him, and vitally knit to Him. This mighty subject, as he looked with indignation on the beggarly system of meats and drinks and hallowed days and angelic mediations to which his Colossians were being drawn down, rose before him in all its length and breadth and height; but as writing to *them*, he was confined to one portion of it, and to setting forth that one portion pointedly and controversially. He could not, consistently with the effect which he would produce on them, dive into the depths of the divine counsels in Christ with regard to them. At every turn, we may well conceive, he would fain have gone out into those wonderful prayers and revelations which would have been so abundant if he had had free scope: but at every turn the spirit bound him to a lower region, and would not let him lose sight of the cautionary matter-of-fact pleading, which forms the ground-tone of this Colossian Epistle. Only in the setting forth of the majesty of Christ's person, so essential to his present aim, does he know no limits to the sublimity of his flight. When he approaches those who are Christ's, the urgency of their conservation, and the duty of marking the contrast to their deceivers, cramps and confines him for the time.

'But the spirit which thus bound him to his

special work while writing to the Colossians, would not let his divine promptings be in vain. While he is labouring with the great subject, and unable to the Colossians to express all he would, his thoughts are turned to another church, lying also in the line which Tychicus and Onesimus would take: a church which he had himself built up stone by stone; to which his affection went largely forth: where if the same baneful influences were making themselves felt, it was but slightly, or not so as to call for special and exclusive treatment. He might pour forth to his Ephesians all the fulness of the Spirit's revelations and promptings, on the great subject of the Spouse and Body of Christ. To them, without being bound to narrow his energies evermore into one line of controversial direction, he might lay forth, as he should be empowered, their foundation in the counsel of the Father, their course in the satisfaction of the Son, their perfection in the work of the Spirit.

'And thus,—as a mere human writer, toiling earnestly and conscientiously towards his point, pares rigidly off the thoughts and words, however deep and beautiful, which spring out of and group around his subject, putting them by and storing them up for more leisure another day: and then on reviewing them, and again awakening the spirit which prompted them, playfully unfolds their germs, and amplifies their suggestions largely, till a work grows beneath his hands more stately and more beautiful than ever that other was, and carrying deeper conviction than it ever wrought:—so, in the higher realms of the fulness of inspiration, may we conceive it to have been with our Apostle. His Epistle to the Colossians is his caution, his argument, his protest: is, so to speak, his working-day toil, his direct pastoral labour: and the other is the flower and bloom of his moments, during those same days of devotion and rest, when *he* wrought not so much in the Spirit, as the Spirit wrought in *him*. So that while we have in the Colossians, system defined, language elaborated, antithesis and logical power, on the surface—we have in the Ephesians the free outflowing of the earnest spirit, —to the mere surface-reader, without system, but to him that delves down into it, in system far deeper and more recondite, and more exquisite: the greatest and most heavenly work of one, whose very imagination was peopled with the things in the heavens, and even his fancy wrapt in the visions of God.

'Thus both Epistles sprung out of one inspiration, one frame of mind; that to the Colossians first, as the task to be done, the protest delivered, the caution given: that to the Ephesians, begotten by the other, but surpassing it: carried on perhaps in some part simultaneously, or immediately consequent. So that we may have in both, many of the same thoughts uttered in the same words: many terms and phrases peculiar to the two Epistles; many instances of the same term or phrase still sounding in the writer's ear, but used in the two in a different connexion. All these are taken by the impugners of the Ephesian Epistle as tokens of its spuriousness: I should rather regard them as psychological phenomena strictly and beautifully corresponding to the circumstances under which we have reason to believe the two Epistles to have been written; and as fresh elucidations of the mental and spiritual character of the great Apostle.'*

It remains that we indicate, as usual, the places in this Epistle requiring correction, either in the readings, or the renderings, of our English version.

In ch. i. 1, as has been already noticed, our two

---

* 'New Testament for English Readers,' Introduction, vol. ii. part ii.

oldest MSS. omit the words 'at Ephesus.' All the rest contain them; and it is probable that they formed a part of the original text. See above. In ver. 6, '*wherein he hath made us accepted,*' should be, 'which he freely bestowed upon us.' In ver. 14, instead of 'who' (masculine), several of our oldest MSS. read 'which' (neuter). In ver. 15, 'the love which ye have' is omitted by our three oldest MSS. In ver. 18, '*understanding*' should be 'heart,' as in all our ancient MSS. In the same verse, for '*and* what,' read 'what.' In ver. 20, some of the most eminent MSS. read 'which he hath wrought.'

In ch. ii. 17, all our oldest authorities read 'of peace to you which were afar off, and of peace to you which were nigh;' and in ver. 19, 'but are fellow-citizens.'

In ch. iii. 3, instead of '*how that by* **revelation** *he made known unto me the mystery*,' read 'that by revelation was the mystery made known unto me.' In ver. 6, for '*his promise in Christ*,' read 'the promise in Christ Jesus.' In ver. 8, for '*preach among the Gentiles the*,' read 'bring to the Gentiles the glad tidings of the.' In ver. 9, for '*fellowship*,' read, with all our most ancient authorities of every kind, 'dispensation.' In ver. 9, omit '*by Jesus*

Christ,' with all our oldest authorities. In ver. 14, omit, with the same, the words '*of our Lord Jesus Christ.*' In ver. 21, for '*in the church by Christ Jesus,*' read '*in the church and in Christ Jesus.*'

In ch. iv. 6, 'in *you* all' should be 'in all.' No ancient MS. reads 'in *you* all;' some have 'in us all,' but the chief read 'in all.' In ver. 9, '*first*' is omitted by the majority of our ancient MSS. In ver. 17, for '*other Gentiles,*' read 'also the Gentiles.'

In ch. v. 2, for 'us' (first time) two of the oldest MSS. read 'you;' and for 'us' (second time) one of the oldest MSS. reads 'you.' In ver. 5, all the ancient authorities have, 'For of this ye are sure, knowing,' &c. In ver. 9, for 'the fruit of the *Spirit,*' all the oldest MSS. have 'the fruit of the light.' In ver. 17, for '*understanding,*' the oldest MSS. have 'understand' (imperative). In ver. 19, 'spiritual' is omitted by one of the oldest MSS. In ver. 21, for '*God,*' read 'Christ.' In ver. 22, it should stand, 'Ye wives, unto your own husbands,' &c. In ver. 23, read, 'As Christ also is the head of the church, himself the Saviour of the body.' In ver. 24, omit '*own.*' In ver. 27, read, with all the oldest MSS., 'that he might himself present unto himself,' &c. After 'men' in ver. 28, and after 'Christ' in ver. 29, insert 'also.' In ver. 30, 'of his flesh and of his bones' is omitted by our three oldest MSS.

In ch. vi. 1, 'in the Lord' is omitted by some of the oldest MSS. Ver. 8 should stand, 'knowing that each man, if he shall have done any good thing, shall receive the same from the Lord,' &c. In ver. 9, for '*your master also,*' read 'their master and yours.' In ver. 10, for '*Finally,*' read 'Henceforth,' and omit 'my brethren.' In ver. 12, for '*the darkness of this world,*' read 'this present darkness.' In ver. 16, for 'above all,' our two oldest MSS. read 'in all things' (see below).

The principal errors and inaccuracies in translation are as follow :—In ch. i. 3, 4, '*hath* blessed' should be 'blessed,' and '*hath* chosen' should be 'chose ;' 'heavenly places' should be 'the heavenly places.' In ver. 5, '*the adoption of children*' should be simply 'adoption ;' and 'to *himself*' should be 'unto him.' In ver. 6, '*the beloved*' would be more clearly expressed by 'the beloved One.' As it stands, it might be plural. In ver. 7, '*sins*' ought to have been 'our transgressions.' In ver. 8, '*wherein he hath abounded*' should have been, 'wherein he made to abound.' In ver. 9, 'he *hath* purposed' should be, 'he purposed.' Ver. 10 should run thus: 'unto the dispensation of the fulness of the times, to gather up all things in Christ,' &c. In ver. 11, '*in whom we also* have obtained an inheritance' should be, 'in whom we were also made his inheritance.' Ver. 12 is ambiguous as it stands in the Authorised Version: 'who first trusted in Christ' may refer to 'we,' or to the person spoken of in 'his glory.' The 'we' should be repeated: 'that we should be to the praise of his glory, we who before have hoped in Christ.' Ver. 13 should stand thus: 'In whom are ye also, having heard the word of truth, the Gospel of your salvation: in whom also ye having believed were sealed by the Spirit of the promise, even the holy Spirit.' In ver. 14, for '*until* the redemption,' read 'for the redemption.' In ver. 15, for '*your faith in the Lord Jesus*,' 'the faith in the Lord Jesus which is among you.' In ver. 17, for 'the knowledge,' read 'full knowledge.' In ver. 19, for '*his mighty power*,' read 'the might of his strength.' In ver. 20, for '*when he raised him*,' 'by raising him.' In ver. 22, for '*hath* put,' &c., 'put all things in subjection under his feet.' In ver. 23, 'filleth all in all' is ambiguous. It should be, filleth 'all things with all things.'

In ch. ii. 1, '*in trespasses and sins*' should be 'by reason of your trespasses and your sins.' In ver. 2, '*children*' should be 'sons.' In ver. 3, that which was meant by '*conversation*' would be better conveyed by 'way of life;' 'of *the flesh* and of *the mind*' should be 'of our flesh and our thoughts;' and '*others*' should be 'the rest.' In ver. 5, '*sins*' should be 'our trespasses;' '*hath* quickened' should be 'quickened;' and '*are* saved,' 'have been saved.' In ver. 6, 'together in heavenly places' should be, 'together with him in the heavenly places.' In ver. 7, '*through* Christ Jesus' should be, 'in Christ Jesus.' In ver. 8, '*are* ye saved' should be, 'have ye been saved.' In ver. 10, '*hath* before *ordained*' should be, 'before prepared.' In ver. 12, '*without* Christ' should be, 'separate from Christ;' and '*promise*' should be, 'the promise.' In ver. 13, for '*sometimes*,' 'aforetime;' and for '*are made nigh by*,' 'have been brought nigh in.' In ver. 14, for '*hath made*,' '*hath broken*,' 'made' and 'brake.' Then it should go on, 'brake down the middle wall of the partition, to wit, the enmity, in his flesh:

abolishing the law of the commandments [consisting] in ordinances.' In ver. 16, for '*by the* cross,' 'through his cross.' In ver. 17, 'preached peace' would be better expressed, 'brought glad tidings of peace.' Ver. 18 should run, 'Because through him we both have our access in one Spirit unto the Father.' In ver. 19, for '*now therefore,*' 'so then;' for 'foreigners,' 'sojourners.' In ver. 21, '*groweth*' would be better expressed by, 'is growing;' and in the next verse, '*are builded,*' which looks like a past perfect tense, by 'are being builded' (present).

In ch. iii. 2, for '*have* heard,' 'heard.' In ver. 4, for '*knowledge,*' 'understanding.' In ver. 5, for '*is* now revealed,' 'hath now been revealed;' and for '*by* the Spirit,' 'in the Spirit.' In ver. 6, for '*should be,*' 'are;' and for '*of* the same body,' 'joined in the same body.' In ver. 8, for '*is,*' 'was.' Ver. 9 should run, 'And to enlighten all men what is,' &c. (see above). In ver. 10, for '*heavenly,*' 'the heavenly;' for '*might,*' 'may;' and for '*by,*' 'through.' In ver. 11, for 'Christ Jesus our Lord,' 'the Christ, even Jesus our Lord.' In ver. 12, it should stand, 'our boldness and our access.' Ver. 15 should run, 'from whom every family in heaven and on earth is named.' The authorised version is an ungrammatical rendering of the original. It is very difficult to convey in English the Apostle's meaning, which depends on a similarity of words in the original; the word for family (*patria*) being derived from that for father (*pater*); that heavenly *Pater*, from whom every *patria* in heaven and on earth derives its name and its laws of being. In ver. 17, '*being rooted and grounded*,' would better be, 'having been rooted and grounded.' In ver. 19, 'that ye may be filled up unto all the fulness of God.' In ver. 20, 21, for '*Now*' . . . and '*glory*,' read 'But' . . . and 'the glory.'

In ch. iv. 1, for '*of* the Lord,' 'in the Lord.' '*Vocation*' simply is 'calling' in the original, and should have been so expressed. In ver. 4, for '*even as ye are called*,' 'as ye also were called.' In ver. 7, for '*is given grace*,' 'was the grace given.' In ver. 8, '*captivity*' should be 'captives,' which is what the word 'captivity,' or 'a captivity,' in the original means. In ver. 11, '*He gave some, apostles*,' &c., should be filled up so as to be intelligible to the English reader, 'He gave some to be apostles,' &c. In ver. 12, '*the ministry*' should be 'ministration.' Ver. 13 should stand, 'till we all

T

attain unto the unity of the faith and of the perfect knowledge of the Son of God, unto the full-grown man,' &c. In ver. 14 it should be, 'tossed as waves, and carried about by every wind of teaching, in the sleight of men, in craftiness that leadeth to the system of error; but being followers of truth in love,' &c. '*Speaking the truth*' is a most inadequate and unfortunate rendering. It is the whole being, not the tongue alone, that is treated of. In ver. 16, '*that which every joint supplieth*' should be 'every joint of the supply:' *i. e.*, 'every one of those joints whereby the system of supply is carried on.' In ver. 18, '*blindness*' is a mistranslation. It should have been 'hardening.' The literal meaning is, 'becoming callous.' In ver. 19, '*have given*' should be 'gave;' and in ver. 20, '*ye have not so learned*,' 'not so did ye learn.' Ver. 21 should stand, 'if indeed it was Him that ye heard, and in Him that ye were taught, according as is truth in Jesus.' In ver. 22 for '*concerning the former conversation*,' which conveys very little meaning to the English reader, substitute 'as concerneth your former way of life.' For '*corrupt according to the deceitful lusts*,' 'corrupting (*i. e.*, becoming corrupt—neuter) according to the lusts of deceit.' In ver. 23, for '*in the spirit,*' 'by the spirit'—'the spirit of your mind' being the Holy Spirit, dwelling in, and being part of your mind. In ver. 24 it should stand, 'which was (or hath been) created after God's image in righteousness and holiness of the truth.' In ver. 25, '*putting away*' should be 'having put away.' In ver. 27, '*give place*' should be 'give occasion.' In ver. 29 read 'whatever is good for the building up of the need.' In ver. 30, for '*are* sealed,' 'were sealed.' In ver. 32, '*hath forgiven*' should be 'forgave.'

In ch. v. 2, for 'hath loved' and 'hath given' should stand 'loved' and 'gave.' In ver. 3, '*once*' should be 'even.' In ver. 4, '*which are not convenient*' would be better expressed, 'things which are not becoming.' In ver. 11, 'but rather reprove them' does not quite express the original words. Better 'but rather even reprove them,' *i.e.*, not only make no terms with them, but even go so far, if it may be, as to become their rebukers. In ver. 13 the translators appear to have mistaken the *voice* of a verb, and thus to have misrepresented the original. It should run thus: 'But all things when they are reproved are made manifest by the light; for everything that is made manifest is light; that is,—the light of your Christian light, which will be by your reproof shed upon these deeds of darkness, will bring them out of darkness into light, for everything, when it is manifested, becomes light. The Ephesians themselves were 'once darkness,' but were now become 'light in the Lord,' having been reproved 'by God's Spirit.' For this reason it will be better in ver. 14 to render instead of '*Christ shall give thee light,*' 'Christ shall shine upon thee,' make thee light. Ver. 15 should stand 'Take heed then how ye walk strictly,' *i. e.*, Take heed of what sort your strict walking is; let it not be foolish and headstrong, ignoring the course of Providence and the necessities of place and time, but in view of God's will, and shaped to suit it. The 'strict walker' is but a fool and a nuisance, unless this be kept in view. The English version misses entirely this important counsel. In ver. 16, '*redeeming the time*' is altogether beside the purpose. The original has 'buying up (the) opportunity,' *i. e.*, of good, wherever it occurs: as the part of him who not only walks strictly, but also does it in wisdom. In ver. 18, again, '*excess*' is quite beside the point, and a mere truism. Who ever doubted, that in drunkenness there is excess? But the word thus rendered means 'ruin,' 'profligacy,' reckless casting away of body and soul. The best rendering would be 'profligacy.' In ver. 24, '*therefore*' ought to be 'nevertheless.' In ver. 26, '*the washing*' is a mistranslation; the word in the original never has that meaning. It signifies the vessel in which the washing takes place, 'the laver,' or 'the font;' '*water*,' again, should be, as in the original, 'the water,' viz., of baptism, which is here spoken of: 'by' should be 'in,' viz., in the power of Christ's word, which made the element into a sacrament. In ver. 28, for '*his wife*' read 'his own wife.'

In ch. vi. 4, '*nurture*' should be 'discipline.' For '*servants*' in ver. 5, 6, it were better to read 'bondmen,' or even 'slaves:' the servants addressed were not *hired*, as ours. And the admonitions apply only as far as that which the two states of life have in common. In ver. 6, the words, 'from the heart' are better taken with what follows, 'from the heart with good will doing service,' and not with what went before. In ver. 9, for '*threatening*,' 'your threatening,' *i. e.*, that which is too common among you. In ver. 10, for '*be strong*,' 'be ye strengthened.' In ver. 12, it should be 'against the spiritual hosts of wickedness in the heavenly places.' In ver. 15, for '*preparation*,' 'readiness.' In ver. 16, for '*above* all,' 'besides all:' and for '*the wicked*,' 'the evil one.' In ver. 19, instead of '*that I may open my mouth boldly to make known*,' 'in the opening of my mouth, to make known with boldness.' In ver. 20, '*bonds*' does not represent the word generally thus rendered, but 'chains.' In ver. 24, for '*sincerity*' read 'incorruption.'

www.ingramcontent.com/pod-product-compliance
Lightning Source LLC
Chambersburg PA
CBHW032104220426
43664CB00008B/1126